CORDO

Contemporary Classics of Children's Literature
Series Editor: Morag Styles

A Guide to the Harry Potter Novels

Contemporary Classics of Children's Literature

Series Editor: Morag Styles

This exciting new series provides a critical discussion of a range of contemporary classics of children's literature from Britain and elsewhere. The contributors are an international team of distinguished educationalists and academics, as well as some of the foremost booksellers, literary journalists and librarians in the field. The work of leading authors and other outstanding fictional texts for young people (popular as well as literary) is considered on a genre or thematic basis. The format for each book includes an in-depth introduction to the key characteristics of the genre, where major works and great precursors are examined, and significant issues and ideas raised by the genre are explored. The series provides an essential reading for those working at undergraduate and higher degree level on children's literature. It avoids jargon and is accessible to interested readers from parents, teachers and other professionals to students and specialists in the field. Contemporary Classics of Children's Literature is a pioneering series, the first of its kind in Britain to give serious attention to the excellent writing produced for children in recent years.

Also available in the series:
Kate Agnew and Geoff Fox: *Children at War*
Geraldine Brennan, Kevin McCarron and Kimberley Reynolds: *Frightening Fiction*
Peter Hunt and Millicent Lenz: *Alternative Worlds in Fantasy Fiction*
Nicholas Tucker and Nikki Gamble: *Family Fictions*

Contemporary Classics of Children's Literature

A GUIDE TO THE HARRY POTTER NOVELS

Julia Eccleshare

continuum
LONDON • NEW YORK

Continuum
The Tower Building
11 York Road
London SE1 7NX

370 Lexington Avenue
New York
NY 10017-6503

www.continuumbooks.com

First published 2002

British Library Cataloguing-in-Publication Data
A catalogue record for this book is available from the British Library.

ISBN 0-8264-5316-3 (hardback)
    0-8264-5317-1 (paperback)

Typeset by BookEns Ltd, Royston, Herts
Printed and bound in Great Britain by Cromwell Press,
Trowbridge, Wiltshire

Contents

Author's Note

Examples of Rowling's text are in the form of paraphrase rather than direct quotation as, unusually, permission has not been granted to quote any passages from the Harry Potter books.

*To my family
for their sustaining enthusiasm
for Harry Potter*

Introduction

When I started to write this book, the news was breaking that the BBC was to clear eight hours of air time on Boxing Day, 26 December 2000, in order to broadcast *Harry Potter and the Philosopher's Stone* in its entirety. Using the version already brilliantly recorded by Stephen Fry it would bring this story afresh to a new generation of children. Controller of Radio Four, Helen Boaden, wanted children to be able to look back and remember the day when they heard this wonderful story.

For the BBC to clear the airwaves of normal broadcasting is a decision of national importance. It was a decision taken swiftly when Princess Diana was killed on 31 August 1997 as a way of keeping the world informed. First breaking news stories and then tributes, commentaries and memories filled the airwaves as the country tried to absorb the shocking and disturbing news.

This time, it was a well-heralded and deliberately taken decision and Boaden was doing it secure in the knowledge that she would get the listening figures she needed to justify it.

It is just another indicator that J. K. Rowling's Harry Potter stories, a half-finished septet of stories for children, have become a world-wide cultural phenomenon.

Now, as I am finishing the book, the papers are full of stories about the failure of bookshops to hold to the embargo on sale of the UK paperback edition of *Harry Potter and the Goblet of Fire* – a further

1,600,000 print run of a book which has already sold over 1,200,000 hardback copies – and there are frequent teasing leaks of clips from the forthcoming film: just a couple more indications that Harry Potter is never out of the news.

How is it that Rowling's ostensibly simple fantasy school stories which engagingly and briefly touch on all the bases of story have so completely won the hearts and heads of child and adult readers all over the world?

Was it just a book of its time? Has the ending of a millennium created a deep-seated need for calm and order when faced with the prospect of new and distant horizons?

Was it the beneficiary of an exceptional marketing campaign which bamboozled otherwise cool-headed and cold-hearted critics into a frenzy of praise?

Was it the construct of a whispering campaign among children themselves who fell in love with the boy hero and his friends, envying their magical lives as set against their own increasingly constrained and protected ones?

Or is there something special that J. K. Rowling does as a writer which marks out *Harry Potter and the Philosopher's Stone* and its existing sequels, let alone the three more that are to come, as books with an appeal that is beyond all others?

One answer is that no book, series or author could ever justify the popular and literary success that separates Rowling from her writing peers. The phenomenon that Harry Potter has become has clouded discussion about what the books really are.

But this is not the fault of Rowling herself who has never made any pretensions or false claims for her stories or for her status as a writer. She recognizes that she was ambitious, even arrogant, in planning a seven-book series when she had nothing as yet published. But all authors need a certain amount of both arrogance and ambition to get published at all. She worked hard to bring off the project, spending five years on planning the plots and refining the characters before she even started the process of writing.

This gives the lie to the well-worn story which dogged her early success: of Rowling writing *Harry Potter and the Philosopher's Stone* in a steamy café in Edinbugh, with her baby asleep in the buggy beside her, as a quick-fix way of making money since she was a single parent. It also fits much more closely to the reality of the books: Rowling is no fly-by-night author. The detail of her plotting alone tells of an understanding of the structure of stories and what it takes to make them hang together.

But even if nothing can justify the exceptional level of Rowling's success, there are some clear reasons why the Harry Potter stories have so gripped the popular imagination. Harry Potter's world is conventional and expected. It is reassuring, providing a cosy model of the world as it might be. Rowling draws on a wide range of story-telling traditions and encompasses many plots but at the heart of the whole lie two key story strands: Harry as orphan, and Harry as hero.

Above all, Rowling has a keen sense of humour and a great desire to entertain. After years of debate as to the purpose of books for children, frequently with an emphasis on the importance of message, it may be that the execution of that simple ambition to entertain is what has made Harry Potter the universal boy hero that he has now become.

PART 1

Background

CHAPTER 1

The Publishing of a Phenomenon

Like most other would-be authors, Joanne Rowling found the path to publication a hard one. The idea for her first book had come to her on a train from Manchester to London and she had spent a good part of the next six years writing it. Financial support and encouragement had come from the Scottish Arts Council which, recognizing Rowling's potential in 1996, gave her a grant of £4000 to help her to keep writing. With this support she finally finished the book and had the sequels clearly planned.

The first agent she sent the book to returned it, and so did the first publisher. On a second attempt, she was taken on by the agent Christopher Little who then spent a year sending the book to different publishers. They duly returned it mostly because they thought it was too long. Little persevered however and sold the book, and the seven-title series it was starting, to Barry Cunningham, then editorial director of Bloomsbury Children's Books.

Cunningham, an experienced and enthusiastic editor with a strong marketing background, was creating a small list of carefully chosen and distinctive books each of which was strongly promoted. His practice was to take on new authors and he had a liking for fantasy. He had already published with a certain amount of success the first in another series, Carol Hughes's *Toots and the Upside Down House* (1996), the strange story of a world in which trendy latter-day fairies walk upside down on ceilings. Joanne Rowling's *Harry Potter and the*

Philosopher's Stone was exactly the kind of popular book he was looking for.

Full of references to mythology and folk and fairy stories, it is the story of an unhappy orphan boy brought up by reluctant relatives who, on his eleventh birthday, learns of his magical destiny and takes up his birthright at the specialist Hogwarts School of Witchcraft and Wizardry. Surrounded by other school-girl witches and boy wizards in an enchanted boarding school where the everyday and the unexpected rub shoulders, Harry begins his magical education and renews his struggle for power against Lord Voldemort or He-Who-Must-Not-Be-Named, the leader of the Powers of Darkness. In their first encounter when Harry was a baby, which Harry only remembers fleetingly in dreams, Voldemort killed his parents, Lily and James Potter, who were much loved and admired for their strength in the fight against the Powers of Darkness. But he failed to kill Harry, leaving him instead with a distinctive, lightning-shaped scar on his forehead. It is Harry's unwitting success in this first encounter, a result of the power of his mother's love, that has marked out his grand destiny in the wizarding world. He is born to be the embodiment of good and to lead the fight against evil.

There is much that is traditional and familiar within children's literature: the combination of an escapist fantasy powered by children, set within the wholesome nostalgia created by the boarding school setting; the Dahlesque beginning; the Tolkien overtones; and the Narnian fantasy sequence in the Forbidden Forest, let alone other more exact points of reference. These include the idea of a school for wizards which had been dealt with in a not dissimilar way by Ursula Le Guin in her distinguished *Earthsea* quartet (1968–90) and, with great popular success for a younger audience, by Jill Murphy in a series of schoolgirl witch stories starting with *The Worst Witch* (1974). Orphaned wizards finding their true destiny also appear in Diana Wynne Jones's *Crestomanci* series (1977–88) in which Gwendolen discovers the truth about her magical powers, but in a domestic rather than a school setting.

In Harry's case the distinction lies in Rowling's blend of all of these and her skill at retelling the familiar in an original way. She is particularly notable for her ability to control the complex plot and to deliver it with an excellent sense of pace, for her attention to detail, for her sense of humour and for the addition of some fizzing magic which turns the familiar into the spectacular.

That it was overlong for a children's book at around 90,000 words did not worry Cunningham. His major concern about his new author and her book was her name. From its title, *Harry Potter and the Philosopher's Stone* looked like a boy's book and Cunningham knew that boys prefer to read books by male rather than female writers. Thus Joanne become J. K. Rowling and the process of establishing the new author and her books began.

It is notoriously difficult to get attention for a new author, so Bloomsbury followed the common practice of sending bound proofs with an accompanying fulsome letter to selected authors, critics and booksellers in the field of children's books to elicit suitable quotes with which to attract the attention of others when the book appeared. Some replied, and on the back of the first edition there appeared:

> 'Splendid stuff! It's got just the right mix of normal life versus magic to make it extra-ordinary and hugely readable' – David Morton of Daisy & Tom, the one-stop children's shop in London.

> 'I just loved this book, it is full of pace and interest and so very funny. There is something about Harry Potter that reminds me of Charlie Bucket in *Charlie and the Chocolate Factory*' – Fiona Waters, Fiona Waters Associates.

> 'Mystery, magic, a spectacular cast of characters and a splendid plot – this is a bold and confident debut from a splendid writer and storyteller' – Lindsey Fraser, Book Trust Scotland.

And quoted across the front from Wendy Cooling, 'A terrific read and a stunning first novel' had been snipped from a much fuller and more telling response which went on to say, 'Joanne Rowling clearly has a remarkable imagination and this splendid first novel leaves me full of anticipation of what she might do next.'

Cunningham had received the support he wanted. Enough of the feel of the book was conveyed through the enthusiasm of those first readers, though much of it is the kind of bland and interchangeable puffing that pre-publicity is liable to produce. Cunningham then selected an artist to illustrate the cover, opting for Thomas Taylor, an illustrator as unknown as Rowling herself. Taylor's cover is as simple and old-fashioned as the story. Low budget, lacking the glossy airbrush style that many big-selling children's titles already had, Taylor produced an innocent image of schoolboy Harry set against the background of the scarlet Hogwarts Express. Random stars dotted about hint at magic. On the back, an image of Dumbledore shows Taylor's inadequate reading of the story (not uncommon in the jacketing of children's books). The image of Dumbledore is of a young-looking wizard, smoking a pipe and clutching a book which might contain spells. He does have a beard and whiskers but they, like his hair, are brown where the text clearly describes Dumbledore's hair as silver, the only thing shining as brightly as the ghosts when seen by Harry for the first time in The Great Hall at Hogwarts. The image was changed for later editions: Dumbledore's hair was adapted into flowing white tresses.

In June 1997 *Harry Potter and the Philosopher's Stone* was published as a paperback original with the above endorsements. Though Rowling had not thought of the book as specifically for children when she wrote it, she came to see it as such and it was originally published entirely for children, without any attempt to attract the kind of 'cross-over' market sometimes achieved by children's books, particularly in the US. The print run was of a standard quantity for a first novel and Cunningham and Bloomsbury hoped that booksellers would read it, get behind it and excite their customers about it.

Having done all they could to promote *Harry Potter and the Philosopher's Stone* before publication, Bloomsbury waited. On publication, as is normal practice with children's books, there was no huge response or review coverage immediately. Living in Edinburgh, Rowling was lucky in having the support of a thriving and committed book community. Waterstone's in Edinburgh promoted the book strongly. There was a praising review in *The Scotsman*, '... *Harry Potter and the Philosopher's Stone* has all the makings of a classic .... Rowling uses classic narrative devices with flair and originality and delivers a complex and demanding plot in the form of a hugely entertaining thriller. She is a first-rate writer for children.'

Gradually other reviews followed. Reviews of children's books in the UK are rarely other than positive, so it is their existence as much as what they say that is important.

Again, locally to Rowling as an author, *The Glasgow Herald* gave an early review pinpointing Harry Potter's immediate and considerable appeal to children: 'I have yet to find a child who can put it down. Magic stuff.' National papers picked the book up later: 'A richly textured first novel given lift-off by an inventive wit' – *The Guardian*, while several pointed out the obvious comparisons with Roald Dahl: 'This is a story full of surprises and jokes; comparisons with Dahl are, this time, justified' – *The Sunday Times*, and '... the most imaginative debut since Roald Dahl' – *The Mail on Sunday*.

The specialist children's book magazine, *Books for Keeps*, also endorsed this new writer. Editor Rosemary Stones selected *Harry Potter and the Philosopher's Stone* for her New Talent column in the issue of September 1997, awarding it four out of a possible five stars. 'A school story for young wizards and witches has been done before but in this ambitious, many-layered, overlong first novel, Rowling creates a fresh and amusing school of magic in which there are lessons in Potions and the History of Magic and rugby is replaced by Quidditch – a kind of polo on broomsticks. The everyday friendships and rivalries of school life give a realistic base to the plot as new boy Harry settles in only to find himself confronted with the power of the evil magician Voldemort who killed his parents when he was a baby. Voldemort is determined to steal the philosopher's stone hidden in the school, thereby acquiring eternal life and riches. In the ensuing adventures, the themes of bravery and the need to understand the "desperate desires of our hearts" are convincingly developed. Rowling is a most exciting and vigorous new talent.'

Adult critics who noticed Rowling's debut recognized her great story-telling strengths and identified her direct appeal to children. It was impossible not to spot similarities with Dahl. They were so obvious that it was difficult to overcome feelings that Rowling had drawn some of the basis of her story directly from him. Harry's demeaning treatment as a servant at the hands of the Dursleys at the beginning of *Harry Potter and the Philosopher's Stone* closely mirrors the experiences of James in Dahl's *James and the Giant Peach* (1961). Similarly, the physically extreme and contrasting descriptions of Vernon and Petunia Dursley are near replicas of the same characteristics of James's fat Aunt Sponge and thin Aunt Spiker: he has hardly any neck but a large moustache, while she is thin and blonde and has a long neck which she uses to help her spy on her neighbours.

But Rowling swiftly established her original invention too. In Harry Potter she had created a child character whose ability to take on adults by adopting adult responsibilities while still remaining essentially child-like was, though reminiscent of the best of Dahl, very much her own creation.

An heir to Dahl had long been looked for. All quirky or imaginative writers since the 1970s had been hailed as 'the next Roald Dahl', but none had come anywhere near succeeding him in terms of popularity with children, though some, like Andrew Davies with his *Marmalade Atkins* titles (1979–84) and Philip Ridley with his grim urban fairy stories such as *Krindlekrax* (1990), *Scribbleboy* (1991) and *Kasper in the Glitter* (1993), had attracted a certain amount of enthusiastic criticism and a dedicated, if small, readership. Dahl died in 1990 but his books continued to dominate bestseller lists. In the months that followed the publication of *Harry Potter and the Philosopher's Stone* in 1997, Waterstone's Bookshops and the BBC ran a poll for the Nation's Favourite Children's Book which was won by Dahl's last major novel, *Matilda* (1988). Of the top ten, a further six were titles by Roald Dahl: *Charlie and the Chocolate Factory* (1964), *The BFG* (1982), *James and the Giant Peach* (1961), *The Witches* (1983), *The Twits* (1980) and *George's Marvellous Medicine* (1981). Indeed, the only book in the top ten published in the last decade was the tenth entry, Jacqueline Wilson's *Double Act* (1996).

Ultimately new books would be needed to take up the gap left by Dahl's death and the British publishing industry profoundly hoped that it would be a British author who supplied them, as the only other large-volume seller in the last years of the century was the American writer R. L. Stine, whose *Point Horror* and *Goosebumps* series had proved equally popular in the UK. Rowling had certainly produced a book which had enough about it in terms of storytelling and style to make her a convincing contender.

Just as the adult critics had noticed the compelling quality of Rowling's storytelling and her ability to appeal to children, so too did the adult judges who picked Rowling out as one of the three authors shortlisted for the 9–11 category of the 1997 Nestlés Smarties Book Prize. A panel of adult judges made up of an author, an illustrator, a publicist and a critic selected *Harry Potter and the Philosopher's Stone* to stand alongside Philip Pullman's *Clockwork* and Henrietta Branford's *Fire, Bed and Bone* to be ranked in order of gold, silver or bronze by the child judges. First novels rarely hit prize shortlists but *Harry Potter and the Philosopher's Stone* had enough original sparks about it to make it stand out.

Once on the shortlist Rowling stood the chance of winning the Gold Award of this prestigious and valuable prize. Voted for by children all over the country, it is a prize much coveted by authors because of the endorsement given by the readers themselves.

The unknown Rowling won the Gold Award by a healthy margin. Not only did this bring considerable media attention but, more importantly, it was the first indication of how much children loved the book. Largely unaffected by the perceived reputation of an author, children voted for the book they liked the best. They loved Rowling's magical world and immediately identified with Harry as the perfect schoolboy hero.

The favourable adult responses to *Harry Potter and the Philosopher's Stone* had put it in the paths of children, but it was winning the

Smarties Gold Award which marked it out as a book which children would respond to passionately. It also gave it a high profile within the first six months of publication, very different from most children's books which take years to become established as successes.

In the next year, 1998, *Harry Potter and the Philosopher's Stone* won all the major children's book awards that were chosen by children: it was the overall winner of the Children's Book Award, winner of the Young Telegraph Paperback of the Year Award, winner of the Birmingham Cable Children's Book Award, and winner of the Sheffield Children's Book Award. It was also shortlisted for prizes chosen by adults, such as the Carnegie Medal and the Guardian Children's Book Prize. It did not win either, though Rowling collected two awards run by the publishing industry itself, given for its unusual and considerable success in terms of sales and profile, rather than for literary merit: the British Book Awards Children's Book of the Year for the book and the Booksellers Association/*The Bookseller* Author of the Year for herself.

Contrary to the general view that Harry Potter was made by media hype, these awards confirm the reality: the origins of its success in the UK lay in children's wholehearted and enthusiastic adoption of it as a book to read and enjoy.

When *Harry Potter and the Philosopher's Stone*, retitled *Harry Potter and the Sorcerer's Stone*, was published in the US it became an immediate sensation. Indication that this might happen had come when the rights to the US edition were bought by Scholastic Inc at the Bologna Book Fair in April 1997 for an initially undisclosed six-figure sum. This was later revealed to be $105,000, an unusually high amount for a children's book, and it caused a stir that led to the first familiar but misleading news stories about Rowling writing in a café while her baby slept.

In 1998, within months of its publication in the US, *Harry Potter and the Sorcerer's Stone* won the School Library Journal Best Book of the Year, the American Library Association Notable Book and Best Book for Young Adults, *Publishers Weekly's* Best Book of the Year, and *Parenting Magazine*'s Book of the Year Award, and also hit the bestseller list in *The New York Times*, the first children's book to do so since E. B. White's *Charlotte's Web* in the 1950s.

The enormous transatlantic success of *Harry Potter and the Philosopher's/Sorcerer's Stone* established Rowling as a major new children's author. In two continents, children had found an author whose books they really wanted to read. The sales figures were exceptional for any book and particularly so for a children's book.

The shift on publication in the US was that adults, too – at least those professionally involved with children and reading – were strongly in support of Harry Potter. Rowling was scooping up the prizes awarded by adults just as much as those voted for by children.

Rowling and her story about Harry Potter had become a phenomenon. From an unknown beginning, the already-planned sequels were to be brought forth into a seemingly never-to-be-satisfied market that could not wait to hear what Harry Potter would do next.

CHAPTER 2

The Changing Writer: from Philosopher's Stone to Goblet of Fire

The Development of the Series

Rowling has written four books in four years, using an adaptation of the original title for each. The result is that 'Harry Potter' is loosely used to describe all four titles as if they were in all respects – except for variations on the storyline – the same.

Two major strands define the overall shape of the books but, behind that, and increasingly as the series progresses, Rowling has an unusual ability to weave stories together, controlling her complex plots with considerable verve. But a story is not good only because of its drama; Rowling is sound in the emotional underpinning of her tales and funny in the telling of them, both of which play a part in absorbing the attention of her readers so completely.

While the major dramatic threads of the story are, at least superficially, derivative and sometimes banal, especially given that the ending of each is predictable, the interleaved twists and turns are extraordinarily sure-footed. Predictability is familiar in children's stories where the world is seen heroically and optimistically with outcomes that are better than could possibly have been expected. How it is achieved is what matters. The sheer drama of each of the Harry Potter titles is compelling, though with each addition to the series Rowling is giving herself the increasingly difficult job of drawing on details from the previous stories to wind into the current one.

The importance and success of children's books as home of the good story had been highlighted by Philip Pullman in his acceptance speech in July 1996 on receiving the 1995 Library Association's Carnegie Medal for *His Dark Materials: Northern Lights*. He claimed that while adult authors concentrate on form and style, children's books have remained true to their origins in storytelling.

Arguments over whether children's books are materially different from adult books except that they are published as such and are generally shorter are hard to resolve. There do tend to be, however, clear conventions within children's books which include the need for a child protagonist and a well-defined sense of right and wrong. One of the major differences is the need for a strong, dramatic plot. Children read more readily for action than they do for mood; their need to know 'what happens next' must be satisfied if they are to become readily engrossed. Pullman sets out to tell a good story – and succeeds. The trilogy *His Dark Materials*, based on the themes of Milton's *Paradise Lost*, is a great story which he tells with verve, vigour and a significant and vital degree of detail.

Successful storytelling in terms of plot is not just about exciting readers and making sure there is an interesting and absorbing storyline which can be followed. It also needs the integrity to make sure readers experience substantial emotional shifts while they read. The role of good plotting, beyond the superficial one of holding attention, is to allow readers to dream and imagine, to grow and travel.

Despite its superficial simplicity, *Harry Potter and the Philosopher's Stone* has the ability to do all of that. Rowling is a captivating storyteller and her skill lies not just in the drama of the obvious narrative but in the meticulous detail of the plots.

For this, she draws on many sources and uses the two most enduring story lines, common to all European literature, to underpin all four Harry Potter titles, adding variations in the detail to the later ones. As an orphan living with uncaring relatives, Harry, from the opening scene of *Harry Potter and the Philosopher's Stone* where they make him cook the breakfast and treat him as an unpaid drudge, fits neatly into the Cinderella tradition. Repeated throughout literature, the possibility of a major life-change, swapping rags for riches, is universally attractive. The potential for such a change is also what drives people to play the National Lottery or enter into TV game shows such as *Who Wants to be a Millionaire?*

For children especially, the underlying principle of Cinderella is alarming yet satisfying. The simplicity of its story line illustrates exactly how many children both see themselves as children and how they would like to see themselves as adults: it allows them to move from a position of dependence, which can feel like drudgery, to one of supremacy. Metaphorically, it allows them to grow up and take control of their own lives.

Like any other Cinderella, when Harry learns of his true identity he not only becomes spiritually richer, he also comes into money. He, who has never even had pocket money, finds his vault at Gringotts is full of wizarding gold. Why his parents were able to leave him so much gold is never explained. It doesn't need to be. Part of Harry's instant new appeal is that he has money. What he lacks in family he can, to some extent, make up for through his ability to buy things.

Rags to riches is just one strand of the instant appeal of Rowling's plot; but Rowling has also given Harry a clear destiny. He is an Arthurian hero: the boy who can pull the sword from the stone and who has a role to play in shaping the future of the world.

Having established Harry firmly as a child whose domestic situation is to change radically, Rowling then introduces a series of dramatic situations which Harry must work through to prove himself in all sorts of ways. Like any good hero, Hergé's Tintin for example, Harry is always on a mission. Rowling makes use of the power of the quest to provide a structure for the narrative drive and to give moral status to those who undertake it.

In this Rowling is wholly traditional and unexceptional. Harry, protected by the singular power of his mother's love which enabled him to survive Voldemort's attack on his parents, represents the forces of good in the fight against Voldemort, leader of the forces of darkness. In this role, Harry is in part symbolic, even taking on the part of sporting hero with his natural prowess at Quidditch. Harry's lack of assumption about his role – his doubts about his self-worth as in his fears about being a Slytherin because he can speak Parseltongue – make him more interesting than the idea of being simply the conduit of 'goodness' might suggest. He is not substantially changed by what happens to him; he continues to act out his part. But Rowling overcomes these limitations as much as possible by her use of intertwined stories of human and magical characteristics, as each of Harry's major tasks is tackled and resolved. The inclusion of magic allows Harry particularly, and his friends to a lesser extent, to be more resourceful and therefore more interesting within their roles as the series develops.

Even though, as the representative of good, Harry will always win through, Rowling is imaginative and forceful in her understanding of children's liking to be rattled by fears which can later be resolved. Rowling is able to create tensions and chilling effects such as the terrors of the Dementors even within the security of a predictable outcome.

Just as Harry's heroic solutions are part-human, part-magical, so are the tasks themselves. Some are mundane, relying on human physical and emotional qualities to resolve them, and some are magical, making use of what Harry learns at Hogwarts.

While Harry's role as an orphan and his relationship with the Dursleys alters little through the first four books of the series – they merely become more ridiculous and he more distant from them as his life in the magical world evolves – his heroic role is developed substantially.

The fact that all four stories, and the three yet to come, had already been planned when *Harry Potter and the Philosopher's Stone* was published, so that they are an integral part of the original conception and not a later addition brought out on the unexpected success of *Harry Potter and the Philosopher's Stone*, adds to the tendency to view the series as a single unit. While obviously unified by many things, most notably the underlying theme of the struggle between good and evil as represented by Harry and Voldemort respectively, they are four very different books reflecting Rowling's development as a writer.

Rowling's rapid transition from an unknown, first-time author to best-seller in the course of her first novel is exceptional. Even when *Harry Potter and the Chamber of Secrets* was published it was loaded with enormous expectation: Rowling had a huge audience of readers who wanted more of the same. By the time *Harry Potter and the Prisoner of Azkaban* came out, a brief two years after the publication of *Harry Potter and the Philosopher's Stone*, the pressure on Rowling had altered from successful author to international media star. Her readership had extended well beyond the traditional children's book market. In the literary world, *Harry Potter and the Prisoner of Azkaban* took on first Thomas Harris's *Hannibal* and then Seamus Heaney's *Beowulf*, the first in a battle over sales figures in which it triumphed, the second for the Whitbread Book of the Year Prize for 2000, in which it lost narrowly (though still scooping the Whitbread Children's Prize).

Either of these feats would be unusual for any book, but they are quite unprecedented for a children's book. And yet, Rowling kept true to her original plan for the series and to her original audience, keeping

Harry Potter and the Prisoner of Azkaban close enough within the framework she had first established to remain beguiling for the children for whom it was primarily intended. She did not yield to the temptation to write for the adults who she knew were reading her books.

Under the glare of such attention, Rowling had little scope to experiment as a writer. She could not afford to take enormous risks with an audience which identified so strongly with the world and characters she had created. The very structure of the series encouraged repetition and similarities between the titles and, in the circumstances, Rowling could have been forgiven for producing more of the same in *Harry Potter and the Prisoner of Azkaban*. Instead, and much to her credit, without detracting from the successful wizard boarding-school structure, she used her creative energy both to create yet more original characters and to spin out an even more complicated plot into which she introduced far greater emotional depth. The darkest of the books to date, *Harry Potter and the Prisoner of Azkaban* shows Rowling as a more serious writer than the first two titles had suggested.

The overwhelming success of *Harry Potter and the Prisoner of Azkaban* raised near-impossible expectations for *Harry Potter and the Goblet of Fire*. Its publication was invested with high drama as the books were embargoed until 11am on Saturday 8 July 2000. Rowling was now writing with the expectation that she must satisfy an expanding adult audience as well as the children who were clamouring to know what happened next. Although *Harry Potter and the Goblet of Fire* follows directly on from the first three titles, it would be remarkable if Rowling had been unaffected by her popular status. Her increased confidence as a writer released her from the confines of the school story so that she had more scope to develop settings, situations and characters. The result is that *Harry Potter and the Goblet of Fire* is less carefully structured than the earlier titles. Instead of a tightly-woven narrative it consists of a series of dramatic set pieces.

But what is lost in dramatic intensity is made up for in Rowling's writing which is both more exuberant and more humorous. She shows new descriptive powers, sharpens her parodies and indulges the development of complicated magical devices. She is also bold about confronting more directly the ultimate danger which Harry has faced since the beginning: death at the hand of Voldemort. Although it is not Harry who dies, Rowling takes the risk of allowing the death of another student, thus indicating the ultimate nature of that conflict.

Harry Potter and the Philosopher's Stone

Harry Potter and the Philosopher's Stone appears, at first glance, predictable, traditional, and above all, derivative. It has a simple plot: the need to prevent the Philosopher's Stone from falling into the wrong hands; a clearly defined morality as the powers of good and evil line up against one another; a cast of stereotypical adult and child characters, including Harry, the familiar orphan who rises above adversity to become a hero.

To achieve its ends, it draws on all genres of writing – fairy story, school story, fantasy, thriller – pooling the best narrative qualities of them all and, in so doing, creating a story full of the classic ingredients of wonder, excitement and surprise with a satisfying and just resolution.

In the creation of Harry himself, Rowling is skilful in establishing a character and the circumstances which shape him. The excesses of Harry's shabby treatment at the hands of the Dursleys are as fantastical in their way as his heroic role once he reaches Hogwarts. While with the Dursleys, Harry is treated as the outsider. He is the one left behind on the birthday treats, not given presents on his own birthday. His fortitude and stoicism in this adversity are well established, marking him out as emotionally robust despite his ill-treatment. He is also invested with enough spirit to fight back against his odious cousin Dudley whenever possible.

Though Harry is in many ways a victim, Rowling is carefully aware of current, heightened sensibilities on all issues of child abuse. Harry is not physically mistreated. The worst he suffers is criticism and neglect. Most of the description of what Harry lacks is set in ironic contrast to the excess in what Dudley has – too many presents, too much food, two bedrooms. The result is that the external manifestations of Harry's ill-treatment are quickly made absurd and so less threatening. Dudley's new school uniform, bought on a special day trip to London, includes a maroon tailcoat, orange knickerbockers, a straw boater and a Smelting Stick, a kind of knobbly stick which Rowling describes as being for use by the boys to hit each other when the teachers aren't looking and, as such, representing good training for later life. The irony of the description dismisses life at Smeltings as both disagreeable and morally unsound. In contrast, Mrs Dursley's ridiculous preparation of Harry's new school uniform, which she attempts to make by dyeing grey some discarded clothes of Dudley's, matters less. The Dursleys are clearly without worth; Harry's mistreatment by them is part of his strength.

Harry is taken from this caricatured realism to his new-found destiny despite the Dursleys' best efforts to stop it. Rowling handles the transition well. Magic is introduced by degrees, from Harry's first letter from Hogwarts which, addressed to 'Mr H. Potter, The Cupboard Under the Stairs', reveals insider-knowledge that immediately alerts the Dursleys that something is up, to the dramatic appearance of Hagrid in the apparently fail-safe hideaway shack on a remote island. Contrasting the developing wit of the unseen magical sender with the panicky, pedestrian responses of the Dursleys serves to accentuate their inadequacies while increasing Harry's status and character.

Rowling, even as a novice writer with a tendency towards a naïve turn of phrase, is a strong storyteller. She tells a simple story deftly, controlling the pace with enough twists and turns to keep readers waiting and guessing. She is able to imply attitudes through well-judged humour rather than preaching. *Harry Potter and the Philosopher's Stone* is a story that is scary and reassuring; funny and full of pathos. It offers rollicking adventure from a setting that is both entirely safe and inventive enough to captivate and entertain. But the story on its own would not be remarkable, although Rowling's control over the plot is impressive. It is strengthened by the underlying messages about racism and tolerance, education and family values that are lightly but securely woven into the fabric of the story.

The magical place that Rowling creates is also well conceived. All good fantasies need a complete 'other' world, and in Hogwarts School and its surroundings – primarily – but also in its urban manifestation, Diagon Alley, Rowling builds a secure environment in which the rules of magic are properly controlled.

In all of these respects *Harry Potter and the Philosopher's Stone* is on familiar ground. What lifts it from the mundane is Rowling's invention and her ability to create entertaining pastiches. The officialdom of schools is mirrored in the equipment list for Hogwarts with its fussy details added in brackets and the headed notepaper with the headmaster's impressive and rather dotty list of qualifications. These allow children to travel readily from what they already know to the invented and magical versions of the same that Rowling creates. Original magical touches too, such as the sorting hat which decides which house a pupil should go into, and the 'alive' portraits which guard the entrance to each house, are also indicators of Rowling's creative flair for invention.

Of all of these, it is with the introduction of Quidditch – a fantasy sport that captures all the necessary details of any sport, blending passions about equipment, teams, ridiculous rules and the enhanced social status of sporting heroes – that Rowling reveals the range of her inventive vocabulary and the extent of her ability to create a sustained and detailed parody. Quaffles, Bludgers, Beaters, the Golden Snitch – the idea of a game with balls that fly directly at players, a scoring system so complex that achieving the main objective can cause a team to lose the game, conducted in three dimensions by teams flying broomsticks – it is an imaginative tour de force.

Having invented the game, Rowling perfectly mimics the obsessive conversations about relative merits of different broomsticks; the loving attention paid to that equipment as when Hermione gives Harry a Broomstick Servicing Kit for his birthday in *Harry Potter and the Prisoner of Azkaban*; the constant need to update equipment; and the status attached to having that equipment. This not only embeds Quidditch in the story but also links it closely enough to all other 'real' sports to make it a recognizable joke which Rowling shares with the reader.

When Harry's innate skill as a Quidditch player, specifically a Seeker, is demonstrated to Professor McGonagall, she rewards him with the gift of a suitably sporty broomstick. Harry's friend Ron Weasley shows his mixture of pride in Harry's surprising skill and envy at the quality of the broomstick by displaying his immediate knowledge of exactly which model it is and in which particular ways it is superior to Draco Malfoy's broomstick. Malfoy's reaction is convincingly jealous in contrast to Ron's awareness that his own lack of a decent broomstick marks out his poverty in a painfully accurate way.

Lee Jordan's sporting commentary on the first Quidditch match – complete with personal and biased asides – is an equally sure parody and provides further endorsement of the fantasy sport which is one of the most successful ingredients of the Harry Potter titles.

If the initial power of *Harry Potter and the Philosopher's Stone* to grip lies in its good storytelling with magical embellishment and its strong sense of place, Rowling's characters, too, have immediate appeal to children. Rescued from his unhappy childhood and transported to Hogwarts and his magical destiny, Harry is the perfect underdog hero. A very British invention, he is an old-fashioned 'everyboy'. In the best tradition of public school literature, Harry courageously but apparently nonchalantly rises above his adversities.

What makes him more appealing is that this comes in spite of his recurring self-doubt which is reinforced by several factors: his ability to speak Parseltongue, the link between his and Voldemort's wands, the Sorting Hat's suggestion that he would have done well in Slytherin. Throughout, Rowling keeps alive the underlying and sinister link between Harry and Voldemort. She is careful not to make him too successful too fast. In *Harry Potter and the Philosopher's Stone* his magic powers are limited. He initially has only the innate magical skills with which he was born. While at the Dursleys' he is able to grow his hair back overnight after Mrs Dursley has sheared it all off in a savage moment when she tires of him coming home from the barber with it as though it hadn't been cut at all. On another occasion, he finds himself high on the school chimney after fleeing to safety from Dudley and his gang. These are small signs of unusual powers. A far greater power is clearly at work when Harry hears the boa constrictor in the zoo speak to him, and shatters the glass allowing it to escape. Armed with this raw and to himself as yet unrecognized magical skill, Harry arrives at Hogwarts where his ignorance of the wizarding world allows him to have the appearance of an innocent, out of his depth and surrounded by those who are more knowing.

In Harry's best friends, Ron Weasley and Hermione Granger, Rowling introduces two characters, again familiar and unoriginal but likeable and easy to identify with. Good-natured Ron is himself lightweight, but he is given substance by his more successful brothers and his 'pure blood' family. Eager, clever, outspoken Hermione is more interesting and provides more entertainment. But the humour is sometimes ill-placed. The jokes against Hermione are about her cleverness, her eagerness to please and her dislike of breaking rules, all of which serve to make a potential heroine into a bit of a prig.

Taken together, Harry, Ron and Hermione make an attractive threesome: exactly the kind of well-intentioned if sometimes petty rule-breaking heroes and heroines that any school or adventure story should have. With a gung-ho, 'all for one, and one for all' mentality they risk house points in the cause of defeating their school enemies, the infamous Malfoy and his two acolytes, Crabbe and Goyle. The risks are magnified, and the rule-breaking more serious, when they take on the greater enemy, Voldemort.

As schoolboy villains, Malfoy, Crabbe and Goyle posture and needle with enough menace to be convincing. Crabbe and Goyle have no individual personalities but their thuggish support for Malfoy stiffens his resolve and emboldens him in his confrontations with Harry. Their taunting of Ron about his poverty, Hermione about her lack of pure blood and Harry out of an unspecific but profound dislike probably caused by jealousy is based closely enough on the reality of any school to be uncomfortably telling. Rowling is restrained in the amount of magical harm the boys can do to each other, making the hostility between the two groups one of human emotion.

Other Hogwarts pupils remain shadowy, except for the Weasley brothers. In the interaction between the likeable, prank-playing twins Fred and George and the pompous Percy, Rowling reveals a good ear for dialogue and for the dynamics of a large family. The twins are genuinely funny, especially in their teasing of Percy: their endless mocking is warm but sharp, exposing exactly what an irritating kind of person Percy is.

If the Hogwarts pupils have clearly defined roles, so too do the Hogwarts teachers. Headmaster Dumbledore is omnipotent and benign. He is the embodiment of supreme goodness, the only real counterweight to the evil of Voldemort. Other teachers are equally representational: Hagrid, misguided but big-hearted, who acts as Harry's mentor and unofficial guardian; Professor McGonagall, the protective head of Gryffindor House; and, representative of all the unjust exercise of authority, Snape. Though largely symbolic, the teachers are sufficiently well-drawn to be interesting.

Rowling's most successfully original characters are the Hogwarts ghosts who are as much part of the school as the teachers themselves. As befits such a hierarchical institution as Hogwarts, the sub-class of ghouls and ghosts is carefully structured with a clear pecking order defined by their past status and skills. Their ghostly characteristics, mostly relating to how they died, make them charmingly ludicrous.

Invented names, picking up on traditional stories, a strong sense of place and a firm grip on the story line are all distinguishing features of Rowling's writing, and are all evident in *Harry Potter and the Philosopher's Stone*. Evident, too, are her occasional lapses in creating the right magical invention. Harry's meeting with the centaurs Firenze, Bane and Ronan in the Forbidden Forest and the symbolism of the dead unicorn stand out as an unusual example of Rowling failing to inject magic into a scene which, closely resembling much of C. S. Lewis, falls surprisingly flat.

Stylistically, Rowling's rich invention in terms of names with their witty and clever associations is not always matched by her writing. She has a tendency to fall back on clichés in passages of description, some of which are then redeemed by the injection of magic.

Harry Potter and the Chamber of Secrets

Rowling conceived *Harry Potter and the Philosopher's Stone* as the first in a seven-book series with each title moving Harry on one school year. This was always an ambitious plan and one fraught with pitfalls since it committed Harry to growing up. Just turning eleven at the beginning of the sequence, the kind of adventures that befall him are suitable both to his own age and to the age of his readers. As the series progresses, Harry must remain the central character and yet he has to develop from an innocent new boy, through adolescence to his final year at school. Initially, this poses little problem: the changes in Harry within the first three volumes are slight. But by the fourth title, *Harry Potter and the Goblet of Fire*, Rowling attempts to make Harry a more convincing teenager, partly by hinting that he might be interested in one of the girls in the year above him – making her seem more unobtainable – and partly by introducing an atmosphere of moody teenage friendships between Harry, Ron and Hermione.

Keeping the interest of the readers of *Harry Potter and the Philosopher's Stone* as the series progresses may prove difficult as may the idea of a group of adolescents indulging in adventures that are essentially childish. So far, Rowling has managed the externals well such as mirroring the structure of real education by introducing more subjects in *Harry Potter and the Prisoner of Azkaban*, exactly as they are introduced in the school curriculum. These help to reinforce the idea of Harry growing up while also keeping the continuity of the parallel worlds.

Sequels can take many forms. Rowling has chosen, in her first two, to follow the structural formula of *Harry Potter and the Philosopher's Stone* almost exactly. Thus in both *Harry Potter and the Chamber of Secrets* and *Harry Potter and the Prisoner of Azkaban* Harry is, again, being ill-treated at the Dursleys. The farcical nature of the Dursleys' repression of Harry is accentuated in each of the subsequent titles with the arrival of new outsiders, equal to the Dursleys in their awfulness. Both provide a suitably disagreeable and morally unsound background from which Harry must escape. Repeating the beginning of the first title in the sequence so closely is reassuring but also runs the risk of monotony. Rowling succeeds in maintaining the reader's interest by making Harry more powerful against the Dursleys because of his newly acquired magical skills and his contact with the magical world, most notably through the arrival of the house elf, Dobby, and by varying his method of escape. She becomes more ambitious in the creation of methods of removing Harry from one world to the other. His rescue by Ron and the

Weasley twins, flying in their father's car which they have 'borrowed', creates a new kind of magic. It also highlights the problems of the interface between the parallel worlds.

Hogwarts initially remains largely unchanged in *Harry Potter and the Chamber of Secrets* and there is the familiar mix of lessons, Quidditch and feuding between the houses, particularly the Gryffindors and Slytherins. There are also increasingly strong ties of friendship and loyalty between the children themselves and with the ghosts. But Rowling adds original new characters and her plot is considerably more ambitious, both in its intricacy and in its development of the dark, underlying racist issues which lie behind it. *Harry Potter and the Chamber of Secrets* lacks the endearing and naïve simplicity of *Harry Potter and the Philosopher's Stone* and has episodes which are unwieldy and unconvincing, but it demonstrates Rowling's ability to write at a greater depth and to scare.

With the arrival of Gilderoy Lockhart as the new Defence Against the Dark Arts teacher, Rowling shows a confidence and freedom to create characters who are not just the embodiment of their positions. Lockhart is a brilliant caricature: the spoof star of *Hello* magazine and the like. From the book list for his course with its run of his own titles, through his devious manoeuvres to be associated with Harry and his spurious advice about the nature of fame, Lockhart is engaging and very funny. He reflects the best of Rowling's wit.

In her development of the ghostly world of Nearly Headless Nick, who isn't allowed to join the Headless Hunt because his head was not entirely severed, Moaning Myrtle, who lives in the girls' bathroom and was killed the last time the chamber was opened, and their companions, Rowling also shows a flair for more original characterization. As with Gilderoy Lockhart, they are funny and show Rowling's capacity to invent and to sustain invention at its best.

With only a year between their publication, Rowling had begun *Harry Potter and the Chamber of Secrets* before the overwhelming success of *Harry Potter and the Philosopher's Stone*. It shows increased confidence as an author: a more ambitious story line which explores the destructive nature of racism, driven by careful plotting; the strengthening of characters through learning; and a marked development in the humour and detail of the original creations such as the gnomes in the Weasleys' garden and the mandrake roots grown by Professor Sprout to produce an antidote to the petrifying curse. It also introduces the underlying premise of the series that both Voldemort and Harry are growing in strength, Voldemort through the range of ciphers he can feed off and Harry through his Hogwarts education.

Harry Potter and the Prisoner of Azkaban

While *Harry Potter and the Chamber of Secrets* is a confident but cautious development of the original, Rowling is far more ambitious in *Harry Potter and the Prisoner of Azkaban*. Given the overwhelming success of *Harry Potter and the Philosopher's Stone*, Rowling could well have written a third title which did little more than reprise the first two.

Instead, she stuck to her intention to age Harry and therefore his adventures, year by year. The result is a much more interesting, more unpredictable and far more sinister story which picks up on the theme of exposing or protecting your inner desire, first raised in *Harry Potter and the Philosopher's Stone*. Hogwarts, once the haven for Harry, is now potentially a place of danger, not only for him but for all the other Hogwarts' pupils. The exceptional powers of Dumbledore must now be used to keep the forces of evil at bay. The magical world is far more complex than it first appeared: the school story framework is no longer driven by jolly japery, with the students sorting out their affairs through petty squabbles, but by deeper issues of loyalty and betrayal and their repercussions through the generations.

As in *Harry Potter and the Chamber of Secrets*, Rowling uses previous Hogwarts pupils, in this case Harry's godfather Sirius Black, to fill in Harry's past and missing family life.

For the sheer complexity of the plot, *Harry Potter and the Prisoner of Azkaban* is most impressive. Rowling's ability to pick up on threads from the previous titles and weave them naturally into the new story gives a substance and density to the sequel that makes it richer and less bland than the original. Even the repetitive aspects of the plot, such as the beginning with Harry at the Dursleys, are lifted to a new plane with the invention of the Knight Bus. With this, Rowling resolves crossing between the two worlds with one of her craziest and most likeable inventions. It rescues Harry from the dark streets after he has run away from the Dursleys and transports him to the safety of Diagon Alley.

The increased sophistication of the characters, too, is marked. Professor Lupin, the most recently recruited Defence Against the Dark Arts teacher, like Gilderoy Lockhart before him, is an inspired invention but, where Lockhart is a witty and well-executed caricature, Professor Lupin is both more cleverly conceived and far more interesting. He combines great inner strength with a deep physical weakness giving him a complex role as one who, through an understanding of his own disability, is able to give strength to others.

The terror the soul-sucking Dementors induce has a chilling edge, not matched in either *Harry Potter and the Philosopher's Stone* or *Harry Potter and the Chamber of Secrets*. Rowling is no longer writing an adventure story in which fear comes from the threat of violence from outside, as in facing the Basilisk in the Chamber of Secrets, but is turning instead to consider the destructive nature of inner terrors. This theme is developed through Professor Lupin's lessons in which the pupils learn to face Boggarts, creatures which take the form most feared by the individual – in Harry's case a Dementor. It represents a marked development of the initial theme of self-knowledge.

In *Harry Potter and the Prisoner of Azkaban* Rowling is commanding in the control she exercises over the whole, still able to captivate through strong storytelling but also capable of making greater demands on her readers.

Harry Potter and the Goblet of Fire

By the time Rowling was writing *Harry Potter and the Goblet of Fire* she had become an international star with a status far beyond the literary world. The media attention surrounding the publication of *Harry Potter and the Prisoner of Azkaban* had in particular put her in a different realm to that of any other contemporary author. All three titles were in best-seller lists, the titles were in print in over 28 languages and, world wide, readers were clamouring for more Harry Potter.

Within Rowling's own scheme of work as laid down at the beginning of the series, Harry, Ron and Hermione are now fourteen. She had to make some changes to substantiate the growing up but she also had to keep the attention of her core readership which was from around eight and upwards.

Harry Potter and the Goblet of Fire is, therefore, a more ambitious book, bringing in many elements from the outside world and with a plot of such complexity that it stretches to the utmost Rowling's skill at weaving together the different strands of story.

Throughout, *Harry Potter and the Goblet of Fire* strikes a different note from the first three titles. Where in *Harry Potter and the Philosopher's Stone* Rowling was drawing on other writers and story sources, she is now self-referring, extending her own inventions and particularly developing her magical language. The word-play introduced through versions of Latin, especially in magic words and phrases, is introduced diffidently in *Harry Potter and the*

Philosopher's Stone, considerably expanded in *Harry Potter and the Prisoner of Azkaban*, and becomes a rich language of its own in *Harry Potter and the Goblet of Fire*.

Characters, places, travel and possibilities are also extended both as the magic is taken outside the enclosed world of Hogwarts and its environment and as so many newcomers are brought into the school. The Triwizard Tournament opens up new possibilities of danger for Harry, some of which come from the exotic creatures he is asked to fight. Where 'Fluffy' in *Harry Potter and the Philosopher's Stone* is recognizable from mythology, the four dragons – the Hungarian Horntail, the Swedish Short-Snout, the Welsh Green and the Chinese Fireball – are Rowling's own. So too are the Grindylows, the savage little water-demons which have to be overcome in the second task of the tournament.

In all of these and in her flamboyant, sometimes nationally stereotypical descriptions of the foreigners at the World Quidditch Cup and those from Durmstrang and Beauxbatons, the foreign schools which visit Hogwarts, Rowling enjoys excess. The result is that, although the substance of the story is sinister, there is a lightness about Rowling's writing that shows just how inventive she can be. As ever, where she keeps her invention close to an original, Rowling shines. Rita Skeeter, the duplicitous journalist who relies on some amusing wizardry to help her, is a brilliantly untrustworthy character in her own right. The destructive effect of Skeeter's fake scoops in *The Daily Prophet* provides a caustic insight into contemporary journalism.

The formulaic opening of the first three titles with Harry suffering at the hands of the Dursleys is replaced by a deadly scene giving background to Voldemort and his growing powers. The danger posed by Voldemort's increasing strength and Harry's ability to resist are now of more importance than the emotional deprivation of Harry's early childhood. This is borne out by the changed emphasis of the story so that Harry's involvement in the Triwizard Tournament is brought about by underhand dealing on Voldemort's part rather than through Harry's own questing instincts. It is played out to the end, through to the final confrontation between Harry and Voldemort in which Harry is in far greater danger than he has been before. Rowling is courageous in ratcheting up Voldemort's power: from opening the Chamber leading to the petrification of Mrs Norris, Colin Creevey, Nearly Headless Nick, Justin Finch-Fletchley and Hermione in *Harry Potter and the Chamber of Secrets* to the death of Cedric Diggory in *Harry Potter and the Goblet of Fire*.

It is in this, more than in the externals of possible girlfriends and moody behaviour, that Rowling successfully allows Harry to grow up and the series to develop as planned. Harry is less the boy from adversity, more an under-aged hero.

It is not only the change of structure that marks *Harry Potter and the Goblet of Fire* as a break with the first three titles. Written at much greater length, it shows Rowling as a far more relaxed writer, indulging herself in long fantasies and more extended feats of humorous imagination. The most obvious of these is the technicolour Quidditch World Cup into which Rowling pours invention after invention, some more successful than others, creating a set piece that is impressive in its intense visual appeal though the sharpness of the detail is missing: there is too much invention at the expense of the meticulous matching of reality which is what has made Quidditch so successful in the previous titles. The teams' mascots, Veelas and Leprechauns respectively for Bulgarian and Irish teams, are excessive – far more than a simple parody of national sporting mascots; the memorabilia and gadgets such as the flashing rosettes and omniocular are unwieldy, needing too much description to succeed. But the simplicity of Krum's brilliant Vronsky Feint takes Rowling back to her best. A close imitation of any sport's best manoeuvres, through it Rowling conveys the skill of an individual sportsman and the climactic effect it has on the match.

Rowling also shows new ambitions as a writer by moving away from the tight framework imposed by the school-story setting. Controlling a larger magical world outside Hogwarts is hard and the frequent need to escape detection by non-wizard people, known as Muggles, through the use of memory charms weakens the sense of magical wonder. Rowling runs into difficulties with the boundaries of the magical world and how it relates to the non-magical one. This in turn creates the need for greater invention in the ways of crossing between the two.

Even back at Hogwarts, Rowling modifies the framework that has previously bound the community together into a much looser structure with the arrival of the visitors from Durmstrang and Beauxbatons. These bring in the world beyond Hogwarts and so weaken the intensity of the enclosed community. There is some return however. The arrival of so many new characters allows Rowling scope for a more varied cast and, especially, for more female characters.

Both in moving events away from Hogwarts and in introducing new characters to Hogwarts, Rowling alters the balance of interest for her readers. In the vast arena of the Quidditch World Cup, Harry, Ron and Hermione are very small and powerless; the magic that is being done around them is all done by adults – when someone unknown releases the Dark Mark, the Ministry wizards are in charge of both the magical and the non-magical world. Back at Hogwarts, the addition of Bagman and Crouch as supervisors of the Triwizard Tournament, the visits to the school from both Charlie Weasley and Percy in his new role in the Department of International Magical Co-operation and, above all, the unexpected romance between Hagrid and Madame Maxime detract from the child-dominated world in which problems are solved by children with advisory help from adults.

The opening up on all of these fronts results in *Harry Potter and the Goblet of Fire* moving in a new direction which separates it from the previous three titles. While Rowling shows increasing skills as a storyteller of great invention creating new magical devices such as the Pensieve and new characters old and young such as Madame Maxime, the Durmstrang champion Victor Krum and, above all, Rita Skeeter, she also reveals an interest in entertaining adult readers directly rather than solely through the adventures of children.

CHAPTER 3

Origins and Influences

Writing for children has always had the two-fold objective of educating while also providing a high level of entertainment. Children need to enjoy reading and, at the same time, adults like to be convinced that they are getting something good out of it. The balance between these two is not constant. It slides around according to current perceptions of childhood and the commercial demands of the market.

The last twenty-five years have seen great change in the children's book market, some of it reflecting changes in education and some of it created by the upsurge of new media. The critical acclaim for the post-war literary children's fiction of writers such as Philippa Pearce, Nina Bawden, William Mayne, Alan Garner and Rosemary Sutcliff confirmed the importance of good writing for children. Jill Paton Walsh, Penelope Lively, Susan Cooper, Joan Aiken, Geraldine McCaughrean and many others including, most recently, Philip Pullman have all maintained the tradition. But these books have always appealed to a minority of readers, just as literary novels for adults, which, while being highly praised, have failed to delight the majority of readers.

The tradition of popular fiction
For a great many years, and especially before comprehensive education, children's popular reading was largely ignored. Books were judged by literary yardsticks and not by their appeal to children;

indeed, too much child-appeal could be seen as enough to devalue the status of a book or its author. If so many children enjoyed reading a book, maybe it was too easy, too unstimulating to be seen as real reading. Thus comics, now regarded as a valuable contribution to developing sophisticated reading of both words and pictures, were dismissed as worthless in terms of reading development. The fact that liking what you read might make you a more enthusiastic reader was not much taken into consideration.

In the absence of the kind of review coverage or book shop promotions that adult novels receive, books for children are currently mostly judged for their usefulness. With an increasing emphasis on raising standards of literacy, attention on what children read is as much concerned with utilitarianism as with pleasure. Popular fiction is largely ignored. And yet children find it.

In the past fifty years there have been two writers whose impact on children's reading has stretched out beyond the normal boundaries. Without mediation from adults, both caught the imagination of children, engaged their attention and so transformed them into readers. These writers are Enid Blyton and Roald Dahl.

Determining exactly what it is that made these authors so much more successful than other writers of their time is almost impossible. They are as different from each other as they are similar in terms of content and style. What they share is that they are loved by children but, for different reasons, are far less popular with adults. Blyton was rejected by the literary establishment on the grounds that she was bland, with stereotypical characters, predictable plots and an unchallenging writing style. Objections to Dahl were more vigorous. His quirky, subversive literature was initially thought too distasteful to be morally suitable for children. Already an established adult novelist, his children's books were first published in the US since British publishers were disquieted by his content and style. But on both sides of the Atlantic and all around the world, his sales were phenomenal as children adored the child-centred storytelling of his most successful titles such as *Charlie and the Chocolate Factory* (1964) and, later, *Danny, the Champion of the World* (1975), *The BFG* (1982), *The Witches* (1983) and *Matilda* (1988).

Slowly and somewhat reluctantly, adult commentators on children's reading came round to Dahl and *The Witches* won the Whitbread Children's Prize in 1985. In contrast, in prizes voted for by children, such as the Children's Book Award, Dahl had already won several years in succession.

Blyton has been dead for over 30 years and Dahl for over ten, but they have remained enduringly popular and, more significantly, they are the two most often cited by adults of different generations as the single author who made them into readers. In terms of volumes of sales, there have been many successful authors such as Dick King-Smith, Anne Fine, Melvin Burgess and most recently, Jacqueline Wilson and Philip Pullman, as well as long-standing series with big sales such as *Animal Ark* and the US imports *Baby-sitters* and, more recently, *Goosebumps* and *Point Horror*. All of these have made a substantial contribution to entertaining and to engaging children's attention with reading but none has had quite the same lasting impact as Blyton or Dahl.

In terms of the scale of the impact which the Harry Potter books have created and the number of children they have brought to reading, Rowling's influence is comparable with Blyton and Dahl. Though *Harry Potter and the Philosopher's Stone* and its sequels, written and still to come, have not yet had the opportunity to prove that they will last in the same way, their overwhelming initial appeal to children is similar.

Blyton wrote over 600 books in many different genres. It is not surprising that the successful hallmarks of some of Blyton's books are also evident in Rowling's writing. Though dismissed as an indifferent writer dependent on a limited and predictable vocabulary, Blyton was an excellent plotter, good at adventure and, above all, skilful in establishing fantasies that children could embellish for themselves. She propelled her stories through their adventures with the plot as the telling force, often leaving the characters as ciphers. Her early fantasy adventures such as *Adventures of the Wishing Chair* (1937) and *The Enchanted Wood* (1939) were inspired by Norse legends from which Blyton created her own invented world. Peopled with human and non-human characters, they were largely non-didactic, simple fun with lots of slapstick good humour about them. Blyton became best known in the 1950s for her *Noddy* stories (1949 onwards) which, by the 1970s, were the prime targets for her detractors on the grounds of racism. She has lasted most successfully as the writer of school story series, *The Naughtiest Girl in the School* (1940 onwards), *St Clare's* (1943 onwards) and *Malory Towers* (1946 onwards).

Rowling's imaginary inventions are more sophisticated than Blyton's and more extensively developed, but her ability to create a world and a fantasy which children can enter so completely is not dissimilar. While Harry Potter himself and, to a lesser extent Ron and Hermione, are characters to identify with, it is the drama of their stories rather than their characterization which binds readers to them.

The world of Hogwarts, a school-story framework that bridges magic and reality so successfully, is recognizable enough to make all children who know school feel both completely at home and constantly entertained by the magical variations which it throws up. It is to enter Hogwarts, as much as to be Harry Potter, that captivates the reader.

Rowling is both more accomplished and more ambitious in the plots of all four of the Harry Potter books to date and especially in *Harry Potter and the Prisoner of Azkaban* and *Harry Potter and the Goblet of Fire* than Blyton ever was. What she shares with her is an exceptional ability to tell complicated stories directly and simply enough to hold the reader's attention. The scale over which Rowling spreads her stories, and especially her skill in picking up threads from previous titles within the series and weaving them into subsequent narratives, makes demands of readers that Blyton never attempted. In this, and in the interweaving of much content in terms of social comment, Rowling is more challenging and interesting than Blyton but, like her, she is able to carry her readers with her. Rowling is unpatronising in her view of children and their capabilities in following several story lines. There is nothing condescending in the writing of the Harry Potter stories. Rowling writes at length with successful changes of pace. Her respect for her readers ensures she never hits an arch note as she unravels her complex plots.

If Blyton's lasting success as a children's writer lies in her ability to entertain children with the simple device of a good story, Dahl's appeal is more complex. Like Blyton he is a gifted story teller, though the strength of his stories lies in their quirky originality, a characteristic far removed from the simple, innocent narrative adventures which underpin hers. Both give their stories a child-centred view of the world. In Blyton, the adventures take place without the interference of adults; adults are almost wholly irrelevant to what happens. This is a common aspect of children's stories but, where John, Susan, Titty and Roger in Arthur Ransome's *Swallows and Amazons* (1930) and subsequent adventures are children playing at being 'grown-up' – taking great responsibility for sailing, camping, lighting fires and the rest as their parents would – Blyton's *Famous Five* and *Secret Seven* behave as children and retain a child's view of the world.

The world of Dahl is significantly different. Adults are around but they are, almost universally, at odds with the children that concern them. Adults sometimes have to be annihilated, as with the Aunts

Spiker and Sponge at the beginning of *James and the Giant Peach*; or at least put in their place as with Matilda's disagreeable and dishonest parents in *Matilda*. There are exceptions: Danny has the most wonderful father in *Danny, the Champion of the World*; the little boy in *The Witches* has an exceptional grandmother; Matilda is saved by her kind and intelligent teacher, Miss Honey. As a commonplace in Dahl's stories, children operate without and against adults. They fulfil their magical adventures by being amazing children, not because they are children taking on adult responsibilities. Like Blyton, Dahl's children remain childlike and removed from adult preoccupations even though they may become all powerful as, in different ways, do James after his transatlantic flight in the Giant Peach, Matilda through her enormous cleverness and Sophie in her friendship with the BFG.

Dahl's appeal to children lies in the power he gives to the children of his stories and the humour with which he outrages traditional sensibilities, turning the norms of the world on their head. Rowling's opening of *Harry Potter and the Philosopher's Stone* draws closely on Dahl. The origins of the loathsome Dursleys come directly from snobbish Dahlesque caricatures of people of limited culture and intelligence. Orphaned Harry Potter comes with immediate Dahl appeal. His inner resilience in the face of domestic adversity shows Rowling's ability to identify with the child's view of a situation. Where Rowling differs from Dahl is that her black comedy is tempered by her view of the world as largely benign.

Like Dahl's, Rowling's children remain children. The school-story setting confirms their status absolutely. At Hogwarts, Harry and his friends behave in the best of school-story traditions, breaking minor – and sometimes major – rules, becoming passionate about sport and having run-ins with teachers. But like Dahl's characters, Harry has special qualities. His magical powers allow him to achieve astonishing things, like being the youngest Seeker in a Quidditch team because of his innate flying skills. They also enable him, with the help of Ron and Hermione, to solve the riddle of the Philosopher's Stone. But they do not prevent him from being a child. Rowling's ability to retain Harry's perspective of his world as she unravels the plot in *Harry Potter and the Philosopher's Stone* is central to its success.

But if Rowling is like Dahl in her ability to speak directly to children through her child characters, she has a different view of children's relationship to adults. Where Dahl is largely subversive in promoting the notion that adults should be neither emulated nor respected, Rowling is fiercely traditional. Charlie Bucket, the eponymous hero of *Charlie and the Chocolate Factory*, learns a little from Willy Wonka, the extraordinary owner of the chocolate factory. But Wonka is essentially an overgrown schoolboy just as the Big Friendly Giant – who turns out to have such good Royalist tendencies – has a child-like simplicity. Harry and his peers, on the other hand, are apprentice wizards, part of a long-established hierarchy in which those who are older and wiser are revered. In the wizarding world in general, even shopkeepers such as the wand maker Mr Ollivander, are awesome because of their accumulated wisdom. Children need to be at school to learn from their teachers who are wise and to be respected. Professor Dumbledore, above all, is revered by the whole community and it is through contact with him, the fount of wisdom, that Harry can become truly wise.

Comparisons with both Blyton and Dahl show that Rowling has particular skills in writing stories that appeal centrally and apparently universally to children, making her, along with them, an author of exceptional influence in shaping children's reading.

School story

Rowling's ability to draw children directly into her books through her dynamic and humorous storytelling is underpinned by her skill in drawing from a wide range of sources. Within the Harry Potter stories, she binds together strands from different genres. Wittingly or unwittingly, she has a magpie's ability to take from individual writers or traditions of literature. Sometimes she is reverential, allowing herself little scope to develop her own writing, and sometimes she is merely imitative. But mostly she adds her own invention and wit to enhance the writing of others.

With Hogwarts itself playing such a central role, *Harry Potter and the Philosopher's Stone* is clearly a school story. Rowling understands the scope offered by a school setting and makes excellent use of it. The double-stranded code of conduct in which some, usually trivial, actions are curtailed by petty school rules and the deduction of house points gives a semblance of order in a world where matters of a much more serious nature – even including life and death – are controlled by the greater forces which work for good and evil. Particularly, and unusually, Rowling supports the very nub of the scholarly ethos – learning and what it can do for you.

School stories provide a complete world in which children are both powerful, at least in small ways, and protected. There are rules and regulations which superficially cramp their activities. However, especially in boarding schools where they are away from home, they are cut off from the emotional support of family which, although it inculcates feelings of loss, can also create freedom from the emotional complexities of parent-child relationships. Instead, their emotional energies are poured into intense friendships and enmities with children their own age and with those who are younger or older. The unbroken physical proximity of children in boarding school heightens the tension of the action. It also allows for the possibility of more things to happen just because there is more time, while the additional hours of the night have the benefit of allowing for darker plotting with a greater element of fear. The enclosed world creates an air of excitement about the details of children's lives, without the distraction of parental interruptions.

Boarding school is an alien experience for the majority of children everywhere, but the idea of it has long appealed in fiction. Rowling fits Hogwarts neatly into the tradition, drawing on conventions of rules, hierarchies, an obsession with sport and much talk of food. The food at Hogwarts is good and plentiful and is an important part of the overall value of the school, whereas historically in fiction it is poor and there is little of it. Physically, with its dramatic setting and castle-like appearance, Hogwarts owes much to the cliff-top Roslyn in Dean Farrer's classic *Eric, or Little by Little* (1858) as well as to Blyton's altogether jollier *Malory Towers* stories. Beyond Hogwarts, the village of Hogsmeade – out of bounds to all below the third year – which is enveloped in the same magic as the school, mirrors the pub life in Thomas Hughes's *Tom Brown's Schooldays* (1857). It is an extension of school life which allows greater freedom and the potential for trouble brought about by mixing with the outside world.

Most school stories are less concerned with the education of the pupils than with their social development. Equally in boys' and girls' school stories, friendship is an all-important theme: individualism is not encouraged in school stories and children who act alone are usually thought to be at best merely 'odd' but sometimes 'sinister', radiating the feeling that they have something to hide. To be alone at boarding school is not a good thing. Friends are often drawn together on the basis of opposites attracting; this means that the weaknesses of one can be compensated by the other's strengths. Just as Jennings befriends Derbishire when they both arrive at Linbury Court Preparatory School in Anthony Buckeridge's *Jennings Goes to School* (1950), the one being outgoing, sporty and optimistic, the other reclusive, studious and anxious, so Harry and Ron become instant friends when they meet on the Hogwarts Express in *Harry Potter and the Philosopher's Stone*. Ron's lack of magical skills is offset by Harry's super-abundance of magic, while Ron's deep knowledge of the wizarding world, and of the minutiae of Hogwarts life in particular, compensates for Harry's sublime ignorance.

The inclusion of Hermione into a threesome with Harry and Ron is also a familiar concept, though mixed-sex friendships are unusual if only because there are few school stories set in a mixed boarding school. Like Harry and Ron, the Marlow twins Nicola and Lawrie who arrive at Kingscote School in Antonia Forest's *Autumn Term* (1948) meet the third of their triumvirate Thalia, or Tim as she is widely known, on the train on the way to school. Threesomes have the advantage of being able to produce three responses to any one situation as do Stalky, Beetle and M'Turk in Rudyard Kipling's *Stalky & Co.* (1899). Throughout the Harry Potter series, Ron and Hermione have entirely different but equally important reactions to the desperate situations in which they and Harry are frequently found. Though Ron is closer to Harry, at least until *Harry Potter and the Goblet of Fire* in which they have a major falling out, it is Hermione's intelligent but cautious advice that is usually right and often, in the end, heeded.

The opposition of rival groups is of as much importance in school stories as the grouping of friends. Rivals play an important role in highlighting the moral high ground occupied by the heroes; the good instincts and actions are reinforced by being thwarted or despised by others. Although Harry and his immediate school arch-enemy Malfoy have deeper reasons to hate one another, their relationship in school fits properly within the school-story framework. Malfoy is also part of a threesome but Crabbe and Goyle are merely thuggish acolytes who encourage and imitate his intemperate behaviour. Unlike Ron and Hermione, they do not have their own views which makes the trio both more shadowy and less powerful. Malfoy creates magical versions of bullying, emulating the notorious Flashman in Hughes's *Tom Brown's Schooldays* as he terrorizes the already over-anxious Neville Longbottom.

Schools are rife with class and wealth distinctions. The role of poor but clever scholarship pupils is recurrent in all pre-Second World War school stories such as Elinor M. Brent-Dyer's *Chalet School* stories (1925 onwards). Rowling takes the theme of wealth and class distinctions into the magical world through the divisions between the children of the old pure-blood wizarding families and those who are first generation, coming to it through something within themselves rather than through inheritance. Here again,

Malfoy's stance serves to show Harry in a better light. Malfoy's dislike of Hermione is founded on pure prejudice because she is not from an old wizard family; he despises Ron because his family is poor. Adopting them as his two best friends shows Harry's tolerance and demonstrates that he is above such limited discrimination.

In the juxtaposition of pro- and anti-Harry teachers, too, Rowling follows school-story conventions. As with Malfoy, there are deeper, historical reasons why Snape hates Harry but his constant sniping at the Gryffindors and his ceaseless docking of house points is similar to the negative responses with which the irascible Mr Wilkins always greets Jennings and Derbishire throughout the Jennings books.

Central to all pre-war girls' school stories is the figure of a ma'm'selle. Brought in to teach French conversation, thought to be important to young girls, these lonely and vulnerable young women are usually the victims of hideous practical jokes or pranks. The pupils think they are exotic because they come from abroad. Their foreignness is expressed through their prettiness and elegance and by the fact that they dress well, showing an un-British vanity which the girls both deplore and envy. Unlike 'real' teachers, they tend to cry easily and break into 'Franglais' when rattled, which they usually are. In Madame Maxime, the statuesque teacher in charge of the visiting Beauxbatons team which arrives at Hogwarts to take part in the Triwizard Contest in *Harry Potter and the Goblet of Fire*, Rowling subverts the stereotype while also adopting many of its characteristics. Madame Maxime is huge – part giant by birth it turns out – but also very attractive. Hagrid falls for her instantly. She is certainly not to be teased or tormented and has considerable authority, as befits a headmistress, but she has some of the characteristics of her more traditional fictional counterparts. She is well dressed – her clothes and jewellery are described in some detail – and even the high-minded Dumbledore is clearly affected by her femininity. While the resident female Hogwarts teachers are mostly professional and business-like even when kind, she is portrayed as more feminine in appearance and as more tender-hearted and emotional.

Rowling's school-story characters would be at home within any school; they have entirely real responses to everyday emotions and they fit readily into the hierarchical relationships on which both real and fictional schools are predicated.

Sport, and its place in making school heroes out of individuals, is an essential part of the school-story convention. Emphasizing both the importance of team commitment and the contribution of individual effort and flair, great sporting moments unite schools or houses in mass outpourings of emotion. Quidditch, one of Rowling's most brilliant inventions, lightly mocks the essentially ludicrous construction of most games while also making use of it as a showcase for Harry's magical supremacy. At Hogwarts, as at any other fictional school, the sports field is a legitimate stage on which to play out emotional power struggles. Rowling's excellent sense of timing enables her to inject tremendous dramatic tension into several Quidditch matches throughout the series, varying the pace of the game as well as the incidents which happen in it quite enough to make the result exciting and somehow surprising even when the structure is largely predictable.

Magical schools

Rowling is by no means the first author to transform the traditional school, or school-story framework, by the addition of magic. In Ursula Le Guin's *A Wizard of Earthsea* quartet (1968–90), the young boy Ged becomes 'prentice' to a great mage before being sent to the School on Roke. But while the Archmage Nemmerle, the Warder of Roke, bears a passing resemblance to Dumbledore and the School has Towers in which the students sleep, *A Wizard of Earthsea* is far less tethered to the realities of school than *Harry Potter and the Philosopher's Stone*.

Miss Cackle's Academy, the school Mildred Hubble attends in Jill Murphy's *The Worst Witch* (1974) and its sequels, like Hogwarts, has the familiar hallmarks of school: strict teachers, homework, tight friendship groups. As at Hogwarts, too, the magic allows for flying, appearing and disappearing and some unusual things happening with pets, all of which is handled with great good humour. While Rowling draws on some of the same magical inventions, *Harry Potter and the Philosopher's Stone* and its sequels are more densely textured stories written with greater shifts of mood and pace.

Outside the confines of the school story, other under-age wizards have learnt their trade through studying under their learned elders. Most notably, the young Wart in T. H. White's *The Sword in the Stone* (1938) is tutored by Merlyn who, like Dumbledore, has all the knowledge of the past at his fingertips.

Part of childhood is the acquisition of knowledge which will, when synthesized, turn into power. In most school stories, lessons are sketched over. Rowling, however, attaches great importance to learning. It is only by learning that Harry will be able to defeat Voldemort. Lessons at Hogwarts are the source of vital information which is then used in real adventures. In *Harry Potter and the*

Philosopher's Stone, Ron uses the Wingardium Leviosa spell, taught by Professor Flitwick, to defeat the troll. Learning through hard work is also emphasized, such as Harry's endless practising of the Summoning Charm with Hermione's help in *Harry Potter and the Goblet of Fire*. His mastery enables him to summon his Firebolt to escape the Hungarian Horntail in the first task of the Triwizard Contest and, even more critical, it allows him to get the Triwizard Cup by using the same spell of 'Accio' to escape from Voldemort. More than that, lessons are vehicles for some of Rowling's best invention, sometimes serious, as with Professor Lupin's conjuring up of Boggarts, sometimes in close parody of reality, as with Professor Binns' dreary History of Magic lessons, and sometimes in wild imagination, as with Hagrid's disastrous lessons both with Buckbeak and with the Blast-Ended Skrewts.

Fantasy worlds

Although the school story provides the over-arching structure of the Harry Potter stories, Rowling also draws on some of the themes common to the major fantasies for children and adults.

The magical world in which Hogwarts exists is a whole creation, just as C. S. Lewis's Narnia, J. R. R. Tolkien's Middle-earth, Ursula Le Guin's Earthsea or J. M. Barrie's Never Never Land. It is enchanted so as to be unnoticed by the non-wizard Muggles and, once inside, it is governed by its own logic. Rowling is careful to keep to the internal rules, never allowing illogical outcomes that can only be reached by magical contrivance. Within such an invented world, animals, plants, scenery and weather all have powers of their own. The Forbidden Forest on the edge of the school grounds provides a home and an arena for magical animals similar to those in Narnia, such as the centaurs and the unicorn. Like the Ents in Middle Earth, the Whomping Willow which viciously attacks all those who come within reach of its branches plays an active part in controlling the environment in which it grows.

In Rowling's invented world the major characters, unlike Tolkien's but like Le Guin's, are human, though some have slight mutations. Hagrid, it is revealed in *Harry Potter and the Goblet of Fire*, is part giant and all the wizards and witches have the potential for excessively long lives. They all can, and sometimes do, appear in the real world without attracting particular attention. Whatever their precise origins, all are capable of being affected by the magic that surrounds them. In *Harry Potter and the Chamber of Secrets* Madam Pomfrey can remake Harry's bones after his dramatic Quidditch accident and Gilderoy Lockhart's failed attempt at repair, and she can undo the Petrification curse. In contrast, child characters, even a child with a destiny as special as Harry's, behave almost entirely humanly. Their magical skills are learnt or acquired and Rowling is careful not to allow them to have powers beyond their status. Harry's ability to become invisible, for example, comes from inheriting his father's Invisibility Cloak and not through any special powers of his own. The ability to 'Apparate', the easiest way to travel between one place and another, is equated to driving in the real world. Older pupils must follow a course to do it and then pass a test.

But because this is a magical world, Rowling also invents a cast of non-human creatures whose abilities and powers extend beyond the possibilities of humans. Some, such as Dumbledore's ever-wise phoenix Fawkes, who provided the tail feathers which control the wands of both Harry and Voldemort, or the unicorn found slain in the Forbidden Forest in *Harry Potter and the Philosopher's Stone* whose blood is gathered by Quirrell to keep Voldemort alive, come from mythology. Emblematic of rebirth and eternal life respectively, both have frequently been used for magical purposes such as in E. Nesbit's *The Phoenix and the Carpet* (1904) and Elizabeth Goudge's *The Little White Horse* (1946). 'Fluffy', the charmingly ill-named dog who guards the Philosopher's Stone, has three heads as does Cerberus the dog who bars the way into the Greek underworld.

Trolls, vampires and werewolves co-exist easily alongside Harry and his school friends when they are within the magic of Hogwarts and its world. In *Harry Potter and the Philosopher's Stone* Rowling's magical creatures are relatively derivative and characterless. As the series progresses, so the cast of extraordinary animals develops. Hagrid's menagerie of outrageous and usually dangerous 'pets' such as the mighty Buckbeak is a wonderful amalgam of creatures from other fantasies put together in an original way. The 'live' garden gnomes that inhabit the Weasley's garden and the self-flagellating house-elves, particularly Dobby and Winky, are inspired additions to any magical cast list.

In the power struggle between Harry and Voldemort as the representatives of the forces of good and evil, Rowling creates her own version of the theme familiar in many fantasies including Susan Cooper's *The Dark is Rising* sequence (1965–1977) and Alan Garner's *Elidor* (1965). In both of these, children engage with dark forces from another world or time. With Harry Potter, the darkness comes from within the world of wizardry itself. To combat it, Harry has to grow in magical skill in order to counter Voldemort's power which itself grows as he feeds off his victims and his supporters.

Unlike in the Narnia stories, Rowling implies no religious overtones. Voldemort is a wizard turned to the bad and Harry has the magical destiny to stand against him and to resist his power. Harry is not a saviour even though he in particular, but also his fellow Hogwarts students, have been chosen to play a part in the magical world in much the same way as the children are chosen in John Wyndham's *The Midwich Cuckoos* (1957), John Christopher's *The Guardians* (1970) and Peter Dickinson's *The Devil's Children* (1970).

Enclosed worlds, the struggle between good and evil, the notion of a chosen few – all of these are themes from a wide range of storytelling traditions which have been adapted in different ways. Fantasy is based on the most traditional and oldest of stories, from dragon slaying onwards, which are then given a new context. So too are the central plot lines of the Harry Potter stories: Harry as orphan, his magical destiny enabling him to survive a modern version of child cruelty, and Harry as hero, fighting the major evil of the powers of darkness and battling with representatives of evil, such as the Basilisk in *Harry Potter and the Chamber of Secrets* and the Hungarian Horntail dragon in *Harry Potter and the Goblet of Fire*. Rowling's skill lies in her interweaving of these different story strands. Her stories reflect an impressive eclecticism which more than makes up for their initial moments of imitation.

The Harry Potter stories are a clever fusion of nostalgia for the school-story tradition, laced with high fantasy themes of good and evil that are brought up to date through discussion of rights and race. The interspersing of contrasting contemporary black comedy and social commentary on the late twentieth century provides both context and access.

PART 2

The World of Harry Potter

CHAPTER 4

The Magical World of Hogwarts

One of the oddities of the Harry Potter stories is the unlikeliness of a boarding school adventure appealing not only to a complete cross section of contemporary British readers, but subsequently to international readers too. Even when they were the backbone of the British education system and an important, character-forming experience for generations of colonial leaders, boarding-schools were only for a tiny landed and upper middle-class minority, yet they were the dominant form of education in children's fiction. In the last quarter of the twentieth century such schools had fallen in number and reputation and their status had changed: the value of home now outweighs the value of manliness; parents and the pupils themselves have voted with their feet by electing for day schools wherever possible. Where they remain, the total incarceration and separation from home that boarding school represented has been abandoned as pupils go home for weekends.

To set a book in such an institution runs strongly against the current vogue for social realism. In general, children's books from the mid-1970s onwards have moved towards inclusiveness, reflecting the lives of as many children as possible. From then on, children from a wider social spectrum and racial mix began to figure on equal terms and in a wide range of titles from authors such as Ruth Thomas, Jan Needle, Bernard Ashley and Robert Leeson among others, making families which had once seemed new like the

Ruggles from Eve Garnett's classic *The Family From One End Street* (1937) and its sequel *Further Adventures of the Family from One End Street* (1956) central to contemporary children's books. In terms of housing, such inclusiveness has meant that run-down terrace houses as in Gillian Cross's *The Runaway* (1979) have replaced the kind of comfortable, middle-class north Oxford setting of Penelope Lively's *The House in Norham Gardens* (1974) or the ramshackle country background of Susan Cooper's fantasy *The Dark is Rising* (1973).

Outside the home, authors have adapted their school environments to reflect the reality of state-school educational provision. For the primary years Gene Kemp set her prize-winning *The Turbulent Term of Tyke Tiler* (1977) in Cricklepit Primary School, a wholly credible school which the majority of contemporary British children would readily recognize, and then followed it with a series of stories such as *Cowie Corby Plays Chicken* (1979) and *Charlie Lewis Plays for Time* (1984) in which the same school provided a real background to act as a link between the stories. Similarly, Allan and Janet Ahlberg's five *The Brick Street Boys* titles (1975–6) made use of a typical city primary school as the point of reference and contact for their characters.

Secondary school stories adapted more slowly, but the success of the television series *Grange Hill* marked the arrival of the comprehensive school as an identifiable background. In contrast to the high profile of Grange Hill itself, comprehensive schools in fiction have mostly been signposted by formulaic references broadly indicating a social and educational mix where violence rules amid a pervading atmosphere of chaos.

The world of Harry Potter and Hogwarts School is in sharp contrast. Both the magical world and even the 'real' world which Harry inhabits with the Dursleys are fantasies. But the origins of the boarding-school setting lie not in fantasy but in an old-fashioned reality that carries with it a great many assumptions about social class and money which, it might have been thought, would have been both alien and alienating to readers.

Surprisingly, the tradition of boarding schools in fiction has always been popular with readers for whom it was unfamiliar. Rowling is drawing not so much on the reality of a contemporary boarding-school education but on the long-established tradition of boarding-school stories. Even when they were first published such stories were as unreal to their contemporary audience as they are to modern readers for whom the popular school stories still in print, such as Enid Blyton's *Malory Towers* and Anthony Buckeridge's *Jennings* series, are as much fantasy as reality. They have an immediate familiarity from children's own school experiences but with elements of surprise and unpredictability that their isolation from everyday life makes credible. The enclosed world of the school creates a perfect miniature universe with rules, hierarchies, goodies and baddies – all removed from intervention from outside. Hogwarts is a perfect example of such an institution and is taken to its greatest extreme. Most parents never come to the school and the pupils are even allowed to stay through the Christmas and Easter holidays. Not only does this protect them for months on end from contact with the 'real' world but it also allows them the necessary amount of time for their extended adventures.

Having taken an established literary form which is already, for most readers, a fantasy, Rowling then adds one more unpredictable factor – magic. Following a convention and then making a significant change is a powerful and liberating literary convention. Joan Aiken's *The Wolves of Willoughby Chase* (1962) and its sequels is a series of historical novels set firmly in the nineteenth century, but a nineteenth century that is made unexpected by the rewriting of the real history of the British monarchy, so that the Stuarts are still on the throne and the Hanoverians never happened. The addition of a rogue element allows for unexpected possibilities.

The Harry Potter books are, therefore, a fantasy school story within the larger fantasy of an invented world where magical things can happen. Both have strong literary precedents which Rowling draws on freely.

This makes it an easily accessible imaginary world. It does not tax the reader by asking for great leaps of invention. The framework is familiar; the detail is changed. Its real purpose is that it allows the complete removal of the wizarding children from the everyday world.

★ ★ ★

Hogwarts is the centrepiece of the Harry Potter series. It captures the imaginations of readers as a place credible enough to identify with, yet mysterious enough to entertain. For readers, just as for Harry, it provides a physical and emotional sanctuary. Returning to Hogwarts at the beginning of every school year is a relief to Harry after the emotional turmoil of the Dursleys and it allows for admission into a safe world predicated on old-fashioned values but spiced up by an element of danger. As in the best school stories, Hogwarts is seen from the pupils' perspective. They are apparently allowed enormous freedom of decision-making, a freedom which Harry uses to great effect; peer rules apply to daily interaction and teachers behave with all the apparent unpredictability of both their real and their fictional counterparts. And yet the reality is that Hogwarts is controlled by adults, notably Dumbledore, making it mostly safe territory.

Despite the roller-coaster of terror that Harry has to grapple with during each school year – a terror which Rowling is escalating successfully and satisfyingly in each story – there is a reassurance inherent in the setting that is comforting to the reader. Safe, conventional and providing regular and complete, year-round care in terms of shelter, feeding and clothing for its pupils, Hogwarts is a physical and emotional safe-haven for children. Its clear school rules with their fixed penalties – house points added or deducted, detentions quickly served and dealt with – provide an ordered and comprehensible structure from which the risks that the magical chaos and danger pose can be tackled.

Bullying, for example, as endemic at Hogwarts as at any other school and made all the more dangerous by the possibilities of magical curses, is kept in check by the inherent morality that runs deeply through the stories and by firm teacher control. Malfoy, arrogant and wealthy, is a perpetual bully. His teasing of Neville Longbottom by stealing his Remembrall in *Harry Potter and the Philosopher's Stone* so enrages Harry that he defies Madam Hooch's instruction, reinforced with the threat of immediate expulsion from Hogwarts if disobeyed, that no one is to fly while she is off the field. By doing so, his natural flying talent is observed by Professor McGonagall and so he becomes an under-age Seeker of the house Quidditch team. There is no punishment of Harry. Malfoy's bullying backfires completely though he escapes without consequence.

Malfoy gets let off less lightly in *Harry Potter and the Goblet of Fire*. Catching Malfoy attacking Harry while his back is turned, Professor Moody turns him into a white ferret which he bounces un-ceremoniously up and down on the floor. Only Professor Snape indulges Malfoy's bullying, frequently deducting house points from the Gryffindors without penalizing Malfoy or the Slytherins at all. Harry's hatred of Snape is much fuelled by this obvious lack of fairness, contrasting with the general desire at Hogwarts to protect all the pupils equally. This preferred kind of order and control built as it is on a highly conventional moral code is immensely reassuring and reinforces children's desire for fair play.

More than that, the common feature of boarding schools of any kind is the children's removal from their parents. Squabbles between friends, though fraught, lack the deeper emotional drama of squabbles within families. Complexities of family life – sibling rivalry, problems of parents' divorce, adapting to new step-parents or step-brothers and sisters – are, in fictional boarding schools at least, all left behind. These are the realities for many children and the bulk of contemporary children's fiction in the last twenty-five years has been concerned with 'addressing' these issues. By creating a witty and exciting world peopled by children who are set well away from this kind of reality, Rowling offers an absorbing alternative riddled with external fears while remaining emotionally reassuring.

Despite its brief existence, Hogwarts is now firmly established in the literary landscape. It lies at the heart of the imaginary world, complete with its own landscape, weather system and ecology, and provides the secure underpinning of the stories. It is the most substantial and sustained example of what Rowling excels at: the ability to create an inventive version of something that already exists by careful attention to the detail and structure of the original. Getting the detail exactly right, rather than just sketching vague outlines, allows for immediate and intimate recognition which, in turn, leads to greater scope for witty invention.

Rowling introduces Hogwarts gradually. First comes the stream of letters on headed note paper with Dumbledore's long and faintly ridiculous list of absurd qualifications such as Order of Merlin, first class. Next, there is the school list. Harry's first encounter with the magical world itself is on his shopping trip to Diagon Alley with Hagrid.

On a smaller scale than Hogwarts, Diagon Alley is one of Rowling's most complete creations. Her magical shopping mall is inventive and shows her sleight of hand that takes the ordinary and familiar, such as a bank or pub, a bookshop or an ice-cream parlour, and turns it into something magical and original. There's Gringotts the bank run by goblins, stuffed full of Galleons, Knuts and Sickles, and the Leaky Cauldron, essential for reviving flagging shoppers. Harry's own equipment list, produced with a flourish by Hagrid, captures the flavour of all such school lists. Full of arbitrary sounding details about exactly what kind of winter cloak with which kind of fastenings and bossy instructions about name tags, it is an early indicator of Rowling's ability at pastiche. Similarly, the set book list, including titles such as Magical Theory by Adalbert Waffling, One Thousand Magical Herbs and Fungi by Phyllida Spore and Magical Drafts and Potions by Arsenius Jigger, marks the origins of Rowling's language play, slipping in Latin origins and punning

English. In the list for other equipment, which includes a wand, a cauldron specified as pewter and of standard size 2, a set of phials, a telescope and a set of brass scales, Rowling introduces the magic side of the learning that Harry will do at Hogwarts. These lists of specialized clothes, books and equipment mark out the new terrain that Harry is about to enter.

Diagon Alley is both Harry's and the reader's entry into the magical world. In creating an old-fashioned shopping street and introducing her first magical characters, Rowling provides a background to Hogwarts which, like Hogsmeade, offers a view of the grown-up wizarding world and plays a useful role in allowing Harry to meet a greater range of his own people and to experience the dark magic that is kept outside Hogwarts.

As befits the historical feel of Hogwarts, Diagon Alley has a Dickensian quaintness both in its physical description and particularly in having shops that are run by respectable but obsequious tradespeople. The Hogwarts pupils are the selected young from within a hierarchical and class-ridden society and, as such, they are there to be served. In a world so reflective of the society it serves it is appropriate that at the school outfitters, Madam Malkin's Robes for All Occasions, Harry has his robes hand-fitted by Madam Malkin herself, pinning up the hem while he stands on a stool, while Malfoy is served by another member of staff; in Ollivanders: Makers of Fine Wands since 382 BC, Mr Ollivander is able to provide an exact account of the wands of every Hogwarts student and to ensure that the wand fits the student appropriately. Like all the best servers of gentlemen, such as P. G. Wodehouse's Jeeves, Ollivander has a kind of power over his masters because he knows more.

Diagon Alley draws on a variety of literary sources, while Hogwarts itself, from its name onwards, is clearly in the tradition of the great British Victorian public schools, both real and fictional.

The combination of towers and turrets, the leaded windows, the cliff-top setting are all familiar physical characteristics of such schools. Emblematically, too, it adheres closely to the popular school traditions with the school being identified by a heraldic crest displayed on a shield accompanied by a Latin motto, *Drago Dormiens Nunquam Titillandus*. Animals represent the houses, each one symbolic of certain virtues: a slippery serpent for the cunning Slytherins, an eagle for the wise Ravenclaws, a badger for the patient and hard-working Hufflepuffs and the rampant lion for the brave and chivalrous Gryffindors; obvious and familiar symbols with instantly recognizable characteristics.

Rowling's school is easily recognized by her readers from its fictional roots and, despite obvious differences, from most of their experiences in modern schools. Rowling's own sense of the school is complete and was carefully shaped at the beginning of the series. She adds little of substance. Instead, she embellishes the most successful ideas. This stability is important in keeping the continuity of the books. The familiarity of the setting provides a secure framework within which the magic can be developed. It also allows scope for the creation of new characters and a number of new plots. Rowling's affection for the school, like Harry's, appears to grow through the books as she becomes increasingly at home in it.

Once in Hogwarts, turrets, vast marble stairways and secret passages convey solidity and reality; ghosts and poltergeists mark the school as magical. But Rowling moves swiftly on from these obvious pointers, creating and fashioning more extravagant magical details. Properly rule-bound, Hogwarts is also a flexible enough place to incorporate changes and developments as the story unfolds.

Some of the best inventions are there from the outset: the magnificent roof of the Great Hall is said to reflect the weather outside, though it also produces its own set pieces. Both act as indicators of the mood of the events taking place and the detail within the Great Hall provides a valuable emotional indicator. On Harry's arrival at Hogwarts and first sighting of the Great Hall it is calm and benign with its own stars glittering in it. As Christmas is celebrated by Dumbledore and the few who remain during the holidays in *Harry Potter and the Chamber of Secrets* it produces a gentle fall of soft, dry snow. In contrast, the heart-shaped confetti falling from a pale blue sky which Gilderoy Lockhart conjures up for Valentine's Day is, like everything else Lockhart enjoys, showy, vulgar and excessive. A quite different mood is created on Harry's first night back at school at the beginning of *Harry Potter and the Goblet of Fire* when the Great Hall imitates the storm raging outside which has already soaked Harry, Ron and Hermione and presages the far greater danger that threatens Harry in this story. By altering the backgrounds to these occasions, Rowling uses magic to transform an everyday, potentially non-magical experience into a magical one.

Mood-enhancing interiors are not original but Rowling's detail is sure and therefore convincing. More original inventions designed to reinforce the deep magic which lies within Hogwarts are the interactive portraits who talk to the pupils as well as taking themselves out of their own frames and off on visits to other people's. First introduced in *Harry Potter and the Philosopher's Stone*, Rowling develops this detail as a motif throughout the series. The Fat Lady who guards the Gryffindor Tower exercises considerable power over the pupils in her house as she knows the details of all their comings and goings, controlling access to their common room and dormitories. Initially passive, she develops a personality of her own, especially when she is injured by Sirius Black in his desperation to reach Scabbers in *Harry Potter and the Prisoner of Azkaban*.

Sir Cadogan, who acts as her stand-in while she is restored, is a more sophisticated development. Having created the picture-guardians, Rowling then gives them greater prominence so that Sir Cadogan takes an active role in the plot by randomly challenging all who come by, yet tamely letting Sirius Black through because he knew the password. Tying down Sir Cadogan to abiding by the password rule so prosaically and correctly, Rowling makes his rollicking duelling all the more of a contrast and so more effective and enjoyable.

In *Harry Potter and the Goblet of Fire*, Rowling describes Violet, the wizened witch who is the first to learn of Harry's surprise inclusion in the Triwizarding Tournament, hopping out of her own picture to visit and gossip with inhabitants of other pictures.

Though bound by the magic that makes it a safe haven from too much evil, much of Hogwarts does not rely on trickery but on Rowling's sense of the power of place to create an atmosphere. Throughout the books, Snape's lessons take place in a gloomy dungeon reflecting his malign character and confirming Harry's sense of suspicion and unease about him. In contrast, Professor Trelawney's Divination lessons, an engagingly airy-fairy mixture of traditional and modern fortune-telling which Harry with his superior wizarding skills and Hermione with her extreme book learning can afford to scorn, are held in a Bohemian attic reached by way of a silvery step ladder let down from a trap door set into the ceiling.

Once in their houses, much of the magic that pervades the rest of the school is laid to rest. Within Gryffindor Tower Harry is protected from the larger destiny that surrounds him and all its attendant risks. He is only with those selected by the Sorting Hat to be Gryffindors on account of their bravery and chivalry: essentially all those who are dedicated to fighting dark magic. Even school ghosts cannot penetrate the security of the houses, thus reducing the possibilities of magic. Inside this safe haven, Rowling reverts to a comforting mixture of traditional boarding-school imagery – from the common room which, with its comfy arm chairs and blazing fire, could come out of any nineteenth-century school story, to more sumptuous and exotic creations such as the four-poster beds in the boys' circular dormitory.

Moments of calm within Gryffindor Tower, which is also a child-only area undisturbed by any adults, allow Harry to indulge in his human emotions. It is in his dormitory, waking in his four-poster bed, that he experiences the excitement and surprise of his first ever pile of Christmas presents in *Harry Potter and the Philosopher's Stone*. The ordinary problems of friendships, and especially the relationships of Harry, Ron and Hermione, are played out most fully in the Gryffindor common room. Magic within the Tower is confined to games playing. There are the prankish games of exploding snap that Fred and George indulge in and the more serious and bizarre games of wizarding chess in which Ron excels. But the pervasive magic that dominates the rest of the school is excluded by the portrait that acts as guardian of the tower.

It is because of this important divide that Sirius Black's intrusion into the Gryffindor Tower when he tries to find Scabbers is so particularly dramatic. Only the extreme importance of catching Scabbers because of the danger he poses could have allowed Sirius to breach the convention by troubling Harry within his dormitory. Just how desperate is his mission is shown by the fact that he slashes the Fat Lady's portrait with a knife in his attempt to gain entry.

Like Gryffindor Tower and the towers belonging to the other houses, the hospital wing is an area in which the pupils are protected from dark magic. Unlike the house towers, the hospital wing is controlled by adults, but only a select handful of adults who are carefully vetted before being admitted. Dumbledore himself has a strong influence over the great magic that is practised in it while the cures are in the hands of the school matron, Madam Pomfrey, who possesses a powerful skill in healing: bones mend in minutes and serious magical accidents can be put right without too much difficulty, as in *Harry Potter and the Chamber of Secrets* when Hermione mistakenly puts the hair of a cat in the polyjuice potion instead a hair from the head of Millicent Bulstrode and finds her face covered with black fur, her eyes yellow and pointed ears growing through her hair.

But dark magic is beyond the immediate cure even of Madam Pomfrey. The petrifying curse which strikes first Filch's cat Mrs Norris, then Colin Creevey and finally, Hermione, in *Harry Potter and the Chamber of Secrets*, needs the production of something extra special. Until the mandrakes mature, Madam Pomfrey can only keep those who have been petrified safe from further harm. Her magic cures are not as powerful as the evil of the dark forces.

The hospital wing allows only for magic that is targeted for a specific purpose; for healing and restoring rather than playing a central part in the larger power struggle between Harry and Voldemort.

Dumbledore's study is in contrast to the magic-free Gryffindor Tower and the protected environment of the hospital wing. Hidden so far within the mysteries of Hogwarts that Harry doesn't even know where it is until his second year at the school, it has within it a deeper magic than pervades any other part of the school buildings. Harry alone enters Dumbledore's study. It is clearly too magic a place for lesser wizards such as Ron and Hermione. It reflects the link of pure magic that exists between Dumbledore and Harry and it is here that Harry gains information which is particular to him and which will help him resist Voldemort. Here he meets Fawkes, Dumbledore's phoenix and the creature who provided the tail feathers at the core of his wand and the wand of Voldemort. Meeting Fawkes is vital to Harry as subsequently Fawkes plays an important role in rescuing him, first when he is trapped facing the Basilisk in the Chamber of Secrets and, again, in *Harry Potter and the Goblet of Fire*, when Fawkes sheds healing tears on the wounds Harry has received from Voldemort at the conclusion of the Triwizard Tournament. More significantly, in *Harry Potter and the Goblet of Fire*, Harry is able to look back into the past in the Pensieve tucked away in Dumbledore's study which allows him to see Dumbledore's thoughts and memories and so find out things about the past which help him to begin to make sense of the present.

Beyond the few detailed rooms, the Hogwarts building, for all its imposing location and substance, is a flexible framework with Rowling allowing herself the indulgence of adding new dimensions to it when the developing plot demands. Secret passages and previously undiscovered staircases are added somewhat indiscriminately.

Riddled with magic, Hogwarts not only allows unlikely things to happen in the present but also has a central role in connecting the present with the past. As the stories unfold in all the follow-up titles, Rowling brings depth to Harry and his story by giving him access to his past and by revealing aspects of why he and Voldemort are locked in a battle between good and evil. When Ginny Weasley opens the Chamber of Secrets she takes the story back to a time 50 years earlier when Voldemort had previously attempted to take control. What happened then explains Hagrid's now precarious and semi-detached relationship with the school while also establishing Dumbledore's long-term reputation for inner strength, judgement of character and goodness.

As important as the general history of the wizarding world that Hogwarts holds at its core is the central role it plays in connecting Harry to his parents. The Mirror of Erised which he finds apparently by chance but, as later revealed, actually as arranged by Dumbledore in *Harry Potter and the Philosopher's Stone* allows him to see his parents for the first time.

More unsettling but also important to Harry's development is the effect of the Dementors in *Harry Potter and the Prisoner of Azkaban*. The Dementors, in their attempt to cause him to drown in his own despair, force Harry to relive his memory of his parents' voices and words before their murder by Voldemort. In the same book Fred and George give Harry the Marauder's Map, stolen from the drawer marked Confiscated and Highly Dangerous in Filch's filing cabinet. Apparently a blank sheet of old parchment, the map comes to life when tapped lightly with a wand and given instructions by a suitably law-breaking student. Its legend reveals that the map was created by Messrs Moony, Wormtail, Padfoot and Prongs, mischief-makers of a previous generation. Initially it is merely useful in allowing Harry to make his way secretly to Hogsmeade through a series of under-ground tunnels. It has the added advantage that the exact position of everyone else in the school is marked and labelled. But the Marauder's Map turns out to have greater significance. As Harry's friendship with Sirius Black develops, he discovers the true identities of Messrs Moony, Wormtail, Padfoot and Prongs. The Marauder's Map provides Harry with yet another contact with his father.

In *Harry Potter and the Goblet of Fire* the arrival at Hogwarts of Professor Moody gives Harry a new piece of the jigsaw about his parents. In his first lesson as the new Defence Against the Dark Arts teacher, Professor Moody teaches Curses, an area of magical education apparently sadly lacking thus far for Harry and his peers. By showing the effect of the three Unforgivable Curses, Professor Moody hopes to arm his pupils with vigilance against attack as well as some methods of repulsion. The curses are demonstrated on spiders. In each, Moody shows just how horrible the effects are and, with the Avada Kedavra curse, having swept the dead spider off the desk, he calmly explains that there is no counter-curse and that only one known person has ever survived it, and that he is sitting in the front of the class.

Harry knew the details of how his parents had tried to protect him from Voldemort because the Dementors had revealed it to him, but he did not know the exact method of their death.

Through these links to the past Harry is able, in human terms, to give himself the emotional base which he has been denied by the Dursleys, while in magical terms they help him to act out his destiny.

The boarding school setting, especially with no breaks for holidays, allows the time to make the action possible. Similarly, the extensive perimeters of Hogwarts, including as they do spacious grounds, the Lake and the Forbidden Forest, Hagrid's house and the village of Hogsmeade, extend the magical world, giving scope for out-of-school interaction but without having to shift back to reality.

Total seclusion allows for magical invention to flourish. As with the Hogwarts building, the grounds are extended and embellished in later titles in the series. Once Harry has arrived at Hogwarts, very little of *Harry Potter and the Philosopher's Stone* takes place outside the school building apart from visits to Hagrid's cabin, the scene in the Forbidden Forest and Quidditch practices and matches. This means Rowling's scope for developing an exterior is limited at this stage to descriptions of the grounds. Here the boarding school with the sweeping lawns stretching down to the Quidditch pitch gives the semblance of normality while the Forbidden Forest adds a magical touch to the other.

The Forbidden Forest as a concept has overtones of Lewis's Narnia, Tolkien's Middle-earth and even A. A. Milne's Hundred Acre Wood. It is a dark and impenetrable space imbued with deep magic; it is a closed space that both protects and threatens the school. Its role in *Harry Potter and the Philosopher's Stone* is limited. Entered only once, when Harry, Neville, Malfoy and Hermione are led by Hagrid on a night-time mission to track down whatever has killed the unicorn, it harbours magic of a more traditional kind, presented as a grand set piece and lacking the inventiveness that surrounds the best of the school magic. In describing Ronan, Bane and Firenze, the centaurs who protect Harry within the Forest and reveal to him the proximity of Voldemort, Rowling adopts a different style, drawing on the fantasy traditions from which such creatures come. Lacking the humour which imbues so much else that Rowling writes, this early foray into the Forbidden Forest is comparatively ponderous.

As the series develops, the Forbidden Forest becomes a better adjunct to the school, providing a natural, outdoors setting that allows for a variety of animal magics, such as when Harry and Ron meet Aragog, the blind leader of the spiders in *Harry Potter and the Chamber of Secrets*.

Related to the Forest but outside it is the Whomping Willow. Of modest importance initially, the Whomping Willow takes on a character of its own in passages reminiscent of Tolkien's Ents, the talking and walking trees in Middle-earth. Harry and Ron's journey to Hogwarts by flying car at the beginning of *Harry Potter and the Chamber of Secrets* ends in the clutches of the Whomping Willow which viciously damages the car, showing its own malevolent power. But the brutish behaviour of the Whomping Willow which lashes out savagely and apparently without provocation becomes less arbitrary and more positive in *Harry Potter and the Prisoner of Azkaban*. Though it still attacks Harry, Ron and Hermione by whipping them across their faces with its branches, it does so for a purpose. It ensures that the Animagus black dog can drag Ron under its roots which guard the underground tunnel that leads them to the Shrieking Shack. The Whomping Willow was planted specifically to allow Lupin, afflicted by the curse of turning into a wolf once a month, to make his way safely to the Shrieking Shack without being stopped and thus proving a danger to someone else.

Though the Forbidden Forest and the magical village of Hogsmeade which lies just beyond the school grounds play bigger roles in *Harry Potter and the Prisoner of Azkaban*, it is not until *Harry Potter and the Goblet of Fire* that the grounds are explored in far greater detail, and extended well beyond their former limits. By the fourth title, the Forbidden Forest is just one of several different outside locations, by now taking on the Shakespearean role of a wood, as used in *A Midsummer Night's Dream*, a place where people are mistaken for each other and which they enter and come out of changed, causing confusion to observers.

The expansion of the Hogwarts grounds in *Harry Potter and the Goblet of Fire* is necessary to accommodate the two teams from Beauxbatons and Durmstrang. Their arrival weakens the cohesion of the school story and the central role the Hogwarts building plays in it. The tension that comes from everyone living within the one space that is the school is dissipated by the incomers. Instead, Rowling creates lavish, but only briefly mentioned separate homes for the two schools: suitably feminine in colour and style, though on a large scale, the Beauxbatons carriage home arrives at Hogwarts through the air, pulled by huge winged horses, while the Durmstrang ship emerges from the depths of the lake as a Marie Celeste apparition with a skeletal and ghostly appearance. These two new fixtures have to be absorbed into the Hogwarts grounds but, since they are not broached by any Hogwarts pupils, they remain insubstantial despite their evident size.

The activity generated by the Triwizard Tournament, with the three tasks taking place within the Hogwarts grounds, extends the magical outdoors. The Lake, for example, is initially only an isolating feature, another way of removing Hogwarts from the real world, which has to be crossed by boat for the new first years in just one of the many Hogwarts initiation rituals – a scene reminiscent of Beatrix Potter's Squirrel Nutkin visiting Owl. In *Harry Potter and the Goblet of Fire* it is given substance both as providing a harbour for the Durmstrang boat and in allowing Rowling to create new creatures – the good-natured Merpeople and the vicious Grindylows – and to develop new magic such as the use of Gillyweed to aid underwater breathing.

Hagrid's house is a caricature well matched to Hagrid himself. The noble savage lives in a primitive home that reflects both his closeness to nature and his deep-rooted honesty. There is no magic within Hagrid's cabin as he has been banned from doing any, a rule which he mostly, though not always, obeys. He even has to cook his own food, often with near disastrous results. In Hagrid's hut, as in the Great Hall, food is produced to comfort. But Hagrid's inedible cakes and powerful drinks served on gigantic plates and in gigantic cups are in marked contrast to the endless stream of mouth-watering meals enjoyed in the Great Hall.

The lack of magic within Hagrid's house makes it a place of deep human emotions, like the Gryffindor tower. Despite being totally trusted by Dumbledore, Hagrid's own magical career is chequered. As a schoolboy he was expelled from Hogwarts which is why he is no longer allowed to use a wand. He also serves a brief sentence in Azkaban. Though clearly lined up in the fight against the Dark Arts, Hagrid is far less one dimensional than the other Hogwarts teachers and, as such, he is able to feel and express more human emotions such as feelings of inadequacy and despair. In Hagrid's cabin there is an emotional intensity and honesty which is largely absent from the rest of Hogwarts; sorrows are drowned in rough-brewed beer, spirits revived in cups of tea. Not surprisingly, therefore, human as opposed to magical dilemmas are brought here to be resolved or, at least, aired. In *Harry Potter and the Prisoner of Azkaban* Hermione discusses her feelings about her work and Ron and Harry's attitude to her with Hagrid. Though Hagrid's role as adviser to the young, especially on matters of friendship, is dubious since he is clearly not brilliant at personal relationships himself, his home makes a restfully non-magical place where these things can be considered.

After the tragic conclusion to the Triwizard Tournament, Harry, with Ron and Hermione in tow, seeks refuge in Hagrid's hut. Hagrid takes them in and, as ever, his first remedy is food and drink. He then offers his simple observations on the power struggle with Voldemort. Hagrid's long association with Hogwarts gives him a wider perspective. By explaining that Voldemort will always be trying to get back but that Dumbledore's greatness will always keep him out, Hagrid is able to comfort Harry and to give him hope for the future.

Hagrid's total and simple faith in Dumbledore is reassuring. After the amount of disguise and double-crossing that has taken place, his plain speaking is a relief. His house, with its properties as a safe haven away from the emotional and practical hurly burly of Hogwarts, is a valuable centre from which to consider the large-scale magic that pervades the rest of the school.

The village of Hogsmeade fits closely into the fictional public-school tradition. Straight out of *Tom Brown's School Days* comes the drinking and the shopping. The idea of somewhere that juniors are not allowed gives it a forbidden feeling and makes it a place where the secrets are seen as adult and more important than the kinds of trivia enjoyed by younger pupils. It only fully takes shape in *Harry Potter and the Prisoner of Azkaban* when Ron and Hermione as third years are at last allowed to visit it and Harry, although without permission, also does so. Before that, in *Harry Potter and the Philosopher's Stone*, Hogsmeade allows for contact with some less shiningly wholesome aspects of the wizarding world such as the shifty character from whom Hagrid wins the illegally-owned dragon's egg which he hatches into Norbert, the Norwegian Ridgeback. The idea of a whole magical village is hinted at but because Harry is not allowed to visit it in the earlier stories its exact powers and possibilities are not defined.

On the first occasion that Harry should have been allowed to visit Hogsmeade he is prevented from doing so by the lack of a permission slip from the Dursleys. Instead, Ron and Hermione go and relate to Harry the astonishing array of jokes on sale in Zonko's joke shop, the magical sweets in Honeydukes and the sublime hot Butterbeer on sale in the Three Broomsticks.

The pub setting, itself a replica of the English country pub with its cheery fire and Madam Rosmerta its attractive barmaid, provides the perfect out-of-school communal territory for Hogwarts teachers and pupils to encounter one another, sometimes directly, sometimes clandestinely. When Harry does get to Hogsmeade through the tunnels revealed to him on the Marauder's Map, he has to hide under the table to avoid being seen by the teachers and so is able to overhear a vital conversation about his parents and their school-time friendship with Sirius Black.

Rowling's ever-increasing confidence and invention as the series develops is given full scope as visits to Hogsmeade become more frequent throughout *Harry Potter and the Prisoner of Azkaban* and *Harry Potter and the Goblet of Fire*. New shops such as the clothes shop Gladrags Wizardwear and wizard suppliers Dervish and Banges are visited.

Hogsmeade is a place of indulgence and treats but it is also a place of danger. The magic in it is not controlled to the same extent that Hogwarts is controlled by Dumbledore's great magic or by the magic ingrained in the building. Because of the deep magic which lies within it, Hogsmeade attracts the full range of magical characters, including extreme manifestations not seen in Hogwarts although they are also encountered in Diagon Alley. Going to Hogsmeade introduces the Hogwarts pupils to a wider social world. After her first visit, Hermione reports back to Harry with a combination of shock and awe that she thinks she saw an ogre there. Hogsmeade itself, for all its inclusion of 'Mudbloods', is 'the only all-wizard village in England' so hags and ghouls are commonplace.

Hogsmeade also provides shelter for Sirius Black after his escape from Azkaban. Hiding out in the Shrieking Shack, deemed the most haunted building in the country, Black, in disguise as a dog, can remain within the wizard world but hidden from the Dementors. In *Harry Potter and the Goblet of Fire* he returns to live in a cave on the outskirts of Hogsmeade. This enables him to meet Harry properly and to set the record straight about his relationship with Harry's parents and his role in their death.

With her extensive magical world, Rowling has created more than could be contained within a traditional school story. The school, with its familiar staff–student hierarchies and its conventional codes of conduct, provides an emotional safe haven that is reassuring. The creation of an outside world increases the scope of the storytelling, the range of the characters and the potential risks.

Rowling's exploration of these is developing with each title in the series, as is necessary as Harry's own horizons grow beyond school.

CHAPTER 5

Escape and Separation

Lewis Carroll's *The Adventures of Alice in Wonderland* (1895) was remarkable for many reasons. In it, Carroll invented a fantasy world complete with a fantastical cast operating under rules created and governed by nonsensical logic. In doing so, he introduced both escapism and fantasy as ingredients in stories for children, concepts that were picked up with remarkable success over the next fifty years by E. Nesbit in *The Wouldbegoods* (1901), Beatrix Potter in *The Tale of Peter Rabbit* (1902), J. M. Barrie in *Peter Pan* (1904) and Kenneth Grahame in *The Wind in the Willows* (1908). Between them, these titles established a new kind of writing for children. This replaced the early purpose of children's books, which was to be instructional, and allowed them, instead, to provide children with the ability to dream and explore.

For the fantasy of Alice's Wonderland adventures to work it had to take place in a world that was clearly separate and different from Alice's everyday world. Alice was removed from her own surroundings by falling down a rabbit hole.

The idea that a child in a story could be removed to another world – except, of course, to some kind of afterlife as in Charles Kingsley's *The Water-Babies* (1863) – was new in children's books and led to a different kind of children's story in which separation from the rules and regulations of everyday is an essential for the success of the story.

Once established, sometimes literally as in the walled garden where Mary learns to love and Colin to walk in Frances Hodgson Burnett's *The Secret Garden* (1911), and sometimes metaphorically as for Alice when she falls down the rabbit hole, these separate worlds permit unimaginable freedoms; freedoms which allow readers to move from the known to the unknown, essential to growing up.

The purpose and results of removal from reality in fiction are many and varied. Geographical isolation, as in William Golding's *The Lord of the Flies* (1954) allows the untamed and uninhabited island itself, as well as its distance from outside intervention, to strip the boys of their learnt restraints with disastrous consequences. In Philippa Pearce's *Tom's Midnight Garden* (1958) the distance between Tom and Hatty is one of time. When Tom steps into the garden it physically remains much the same but in another time. Tom goes back into Hatty's time. But, while Hatty grows old during the period of Tom's nightly visits, Tom's own time remains unchanged. For him, the growing older is in terms of emotional development rather than chronological years.

For a self-contained world to exist convincingly, it is usually constrained within some physical boundaries. Where two worlds connect and relate, there needs to be access and the process of removal – the journey – can be an important part of the story. Where both worlds are real, the method of access reflects the mood of the story. In *The Lord of the Flies*, the brutality of a crashed plane in which all the adults are killed is a suitably violent arrival for the subsequent destructive behaviour. In *Tom's Midnight Garden*, a locked door, easily opened by Tom with the key that is already in the lock, reflects Tom's comfortable access to another time and the proximity of Hatty's world.

The successful invention of methods of entry to a magical world is equally important both in defining an atmosphere and in making the transition convincing and likeable. For Peter, Susan, Edmund and Lucy in C. S. Lewis's *The Lion, the Witch and the Wardrobe*, access to Narnia is through the wardrobe while in E. Nesbit's *The Phoenix and the Carpet* (1904), Robert, Anthea, Jane and Cyril take off on the magic carpet for their adventures, returning to the security of their home in between each. Both reflect the very domestic nature of the original settings and make use of a homely piece of furniture to act as the method of transport. John, Wendy and Michael in *Peter Pan* also leave from a very comfortable and domestic setting but their night flight from their bedroom has overtones of abduction about it as they are led off by Peter Pan to his enchanted Never Never Land.

In these human–based fantasies, the new worlds lie adjacent to reality; children can slip from one to the other and must, therefore, be able to exist convincingly in both. This is a kind of fantasy far removed from the invented whole that is J. R. R. Tolkien's Middle-earth which first appeared in *The Hobbit* (1937) and subsequently in *The Lord of the Rings* trilogy (1954–55) and its accompanying volume *The Silmarillion* (1977).

Like Lewis's and Nesbit's children, Harry Potter and his friends must be transported from one world to another. Rowling's real and magical worlds are closely interwoven – the magical areas are more like protected zones wreathed by some enchantment than completely separate worlds and movement between the two is both ways. For Harry the central shift is moving from his hated home with the Dursleys to Hogwarts where he can enjoy the freedom of his true heritage in the magical world. But magic and magical characters can operate in the human world and can invade it readily just as the Psammead can arrive in a bedroom in Nesbit's *Five Children and It* (1902). This is in stark contrast to the largely self-contained country of Narnia which is kept separate apart from the brief and surprising visit of the witch to London in *The Magician's Nephew*.

Rowling uses a number of methods of entry and exit between her two worlds with varying degrees of success. Like others before her, she adopts the ideas both of crossing through barriers and of distinctive methods of transport to make the journey to another place. These mark out the space between the world Harry is living in and the enclosed world of Hogwarts or any of its magical surrounds which he is entering.

Not as domestic or quite as everyday as a wardrobe or a carpet, her main point of entry – platform nine and three-quarters at King's Cross – though clearly fanciful, is nonetheless rooted firmly in a modern railway station. Its public location, rather than the privacy of a domestic interior point of access, makes it a more social and less personal fantasy at the outset. There is no sense of a dreamy child lost in his own world about the Harry Potter stories.

Casually barging through the barrier between platforms nine and ten on King's Cross station is a witty entry to the magical world. It has to be done carefully to avoid impacting on the ordinary public who are left on the normal King's Cross station. Train travel as fantasy transport is both modern – certainly as compared with Nesbit's magic carpet – and has historical overtones at a time when either faster collective transport such as flying or more personalized transport such as the car are the norm. Rowling's train travel becomes more timeless once the barrier is crossed; the Hogwarts Express is steam powered – a train from the past, taking pupils on a long journey which, with all its old-fashioned structure and values, could be back in time too.

Throughout the Harry Potter books, Rowling has added different ways of moving between the two worlds that Harry inhabits. While in all four books the main access to Hogwarts itself remains constant – the Hogwarts Express – there is enough unpredictability and variation to make it fresh. At the beginning of Harry's second year at Hogwarts, Harry and Ron fail to get through at all after the barrier has been tampered with by Dobby.

The scene-setting at the beginning of each title provides vital information about Harry's true nature and destiny – such as his remarkable survival and the revelation that he can speak Parseltongue in *Harry Potter and the Philosopher's Stone*, and the sighting of the Grim (which turns out to be Sirius Black) in *Harry Potter and the Prisoner of Azkaban*. But it is the moment of crossing through the magical barrier at King's Cross that marks the beginning of the now familiar and safe core territory of the books: Hogwarts.

Set in a public place but leading to the private wizarding world, the barrier that conceals platform nine and three quarters marks a clear divide between the two worlds. Mr and Mrs Weasley, fully of the wizarding world themselves, can come through and say goodbye from the platform as can Neville Longbottom's distinguished witch grandmother; Hermione's non-magical dentist father and mother must say goodbye to her at the barrier.

The platform is invisible to the unwitting. When Uncle Vernon takes Harry to King's Cross to catch his first Hogwarts Express in *Harry Potter and the Philosopher's Stone*, it confirms his previous mockery of the very existence of such a platform. Much to Harry's surprise, Uncle Vernon loads his trunk onto a trolley and takes it right onto the station rather than leaving him to manage on his own. When they get there Harry soon realizes why. Stopping between platforms nine and ten, Uncle Vernon sneeringly points out the absence of platform nine and three quarters. He then abandons Harry who has to find the platform for himself. The Dursleys are so hostile to the idea of Harry's other life that they are completely excluded from the secrets that hide Hogwarts. Harry only finds where he is to go by asking Mrs Weasley when he sees her on the platform. An old hand at it, Mrs Weasley explains the technique of walking straight at the barrier without stopping or being scared. She even suggests running at it to make sure, if he's nervous. Following her advice, Harry charges the barrier with his trolley, in terror – but with success.

Behind the clear physical barrier, at the platform waits the means of transport which is a similar mixture of the real and the fantastical. The gleaming red steam engine that pulls the Hogwarts Express is in contrast with the contemporary 125s which are clearly visible on the other platforms. The piling of possessions into the carriages and the farewells to parents are wholly reminiscent of all school trains, real and fictional, with parents offering nuggets of useful advice about harder work and good behaviour. The only give-away that the pupils are off to an altogether different kind of school is the presence of numerous owls and other creatures. The train itself is unexceptional but it soon becomes clear that the Hogwarts pupils – and staff when Professor Lupin travels with them to take up his post as Defence Against the Dark Arts teacher in *Harry Potter and the Prisoner of Azkaban* – are on no ordinary train when they are served Bertie Bott's Every Flavour Beans and Cauldron Cakes from the trolley. Here, as in so many other places, Rowling's slight adaptation of a familiar and pedestrian external into something magical and unusual highlights her invention while ensuring that its basis is secure.

The train journey from King's Cross to Hogwarts is a long one in both distance and time. The train straddles the two worlds. Each journey allows Harry to shake off his non-magical self and to become re-identified with his other world. The journey takes the best part of a day, with Harry and his contemporaries contained in a confined space. On their first trip this allows for the rapidly forged friendship between Harry and Ron as well as the immediate enmity with Malfoy and his cronies. But the train is not bound by either the strong magic or the strong rules of school. Harry is less protected on the train than he is once he gets to Hogwarts. It is on the journey back to school at the beginning of *Harry Potter and the Prisoner of Azkaban* that he first discovers his vulnerability to the Dementors. Though kept out of the school at Dumbledore's insistence, the Dementors board the train having stopped it and plunged it into darkness.

Harry's first glimpse of a Dementor is in the flickering light provided by Professor Lupin. It is instantly sinister and terrifying. Huge, reaching almost to the ceiling, its face is shrouded by an enormous hood and its body is enveloped by a cloak. What first chills Harry is seeing a glimpse of a scabbed hand just visible under the cloak. But worse follows when the Dementor's breath starts to rattle as if it is sucking more than air from its surroundings. Harry finds himself drowning in icy cold with a roaring in his ears through which he hears the terrified and pleading screams of someone whom he is powerless to help. The similarity with Tolkien's Black Riders is evident.

Rowling makes skilful use of the train as hybrid territory. It is the welcome means of Harry escaping from the Dursleys but it also reveals Harry's vulnerability within the magical world and shows the extent to which he is protected by Dumbledore. This confirms the role of Hogwarts as both a physical and an emotional safe haven.

The other methods of movement between wizard and Muggle worlds and within the wizard world itself, apart from the Knight Bus, are less significant as places where things happen and less rich emotionally, but they allow Rowling scope for invention and the opportunity to introduce devices which become important to the plot.

This is partly because Rowling blurs the entry points between the two worlds. There are no clear barriers that separate the areas of magic from the rest. Instead, she allows her worlds to overlap which creates problems of identification and distinction between the worlds the wizards and the Muggles live in. While wizards can move freely in the real world, Muggles cannot gain access to the magical one. But even that apparently sound rule does not always apply. Complete confusion reigns at the Quidditch World Cup in *Harry Potter and the Goblet of Fire* when reality and magic coexist in the same time and space. Through Mr Weasley's explanation to his family and Harry about how a deserted moor has been set up with as many anti-Muggle precautions as possible in an attempt to make a secret place where 100,000 wizards can get together, Rowling indicates that an enclosed zone on this scale is a difficult thing to pull off. The intermingling of wizards and Muggles is necessary to illustrate the pernicious racism and absolute depravity of the Death Eaters when they humiliate the Roberts family by levitating them, but the frequent use of 'memory modification' as a way of preventing the Muggles from remembering what has happened becomes an unsatisfactory escape clause.

Lack of definition also surrounds the Weasleys' home. In every respect the exact opposite of the Dursleys' home at 4 Privet Drive, like Hogwarts it provides an emotional retreat for Harry. But unlike the school it is not within an enchanted world, it is merely an enchanted house and garden. Full of magic inside and out with a garden full of magical gnomes and a hidden area for Quidditch practice, it can also be reached by an ordinary taxi when the Hogwarts pupils need to be taken to King's Cross for the start of a new term. It also appears to lie in the ordinary countryside when the Weasleys with Harry and Hermione set off to find the Portkey that will transport them to the Quidditch World Cup.

Rowling largely overcomes the problem of the blurred barriers between the two worlds by the creation of some original inventions, particularly in her methods of transport. Lacking the coherent logical underpinning of a clear distinction of time or place, their success lies in Rowling's ability to invent and imagine.

To confirm Harry's emotional plight with the Dursleys, he is rescued from his misery in Privet Drive at the beginning of *Harry Potter and the Chamber of Secrets* by being snatched from his bedroom windowsill out of the clutches of Uncle Vernon by Ron, Fred and George flying their father's car. When he runs away from the fiasco of a Privet Drive dinner party at the beginning of *Harry Potter and the Prisoner of Azkaban* he is picked up by the Knight Bus. Both happen at night, which allows Rowling to beg the question of exactly where the two worlds join and part. Fred and George argue that the dark and the clouds would make them invisible to people, and Ron and Harry adopt the same line when they fly themselves to Hogwarts in *Harry Potter and the Chamber of Secrets* but they are seen by humans and Mr Weasley has to adopt some Ministry of Magic techniques to make people forget that they saw a flying car.

While Mr Weasley's turquoise Ford Anglia is little more than a pleasing development of Ian Fleming's famous flying car 'Chitty Chitty Bang Bang' or any number of cartoon imitators, the Knight Bus is an engagingly rounded and original invention from its punning title to its gossiping driver and conductor. Travelling through the night, it seems more convincing that problems of Muggle recognition do not arise and it allows Rowling to indulge in some inventive, over-the-top kinds of magic as trees, lamp-posts and even buildings move out of the way of the bus. The triple-decker bus, like the Hogwarts Express, is a magical adaptation of a familiar original. Its wealth of ridiculous extras – brass-bedsteads, hot chocolate which pours all over the pillow – and its erratic leaping route all over the United Kingdom reflect Rowling's increased sureness of touch and freedom to embellish in *Harry Potter and the Prisoner of Azkaban*. The bus journey itself, which takes Harry from despair at his down-trodden life with the Dursleys to a punishment-free welcome by the Minister of Magic himself in Diagon Alley, is like the journeys back to school on the Hogwarts Express; a valuable space between the two worlds. Unlike at Hogwarts where his identity is known to all, on the Knight Bus he passes himself off as Neville Longbottom and so has an unusual opportunity to find out things which are important to him without attracting the attention that attaches to his destiny. It is here that Harry discovers that Sirius Black has escaped from Azkaban and learns the popular version of why he was arrested and imprisoned.

As the stories become more complex and more ambitious, so Rowling's landscape has grown and the need for interaction increased. Though the shape of each school year provides the over-arching timeframe and the social hierarchies of the school remain the central context, Rowling is moving beyond that narrow confine.

However, for the central emotional core of Harry's unhappy life to be juxtaposed with the happiness that is life at Hogwarts or for him to grow sufficiently in wizarding powers to fulfil his destiny in contrast with his lowly status with the Dursleys, separation between the two worlds remains vital. While Rowling has for the most part successfully enlarged the boundaries of Hogwarts physically, emotionally and with the addition of new characters, the scope for ridiculing the Dursleys remains limited and Harry's constraint by them might in future books become increasingly unconvincing.

In the first three titles, Harry escapes from the Dursleys on his own journeys that will lead him to Hogwarts without the Dursleys having to engage very much with the differences of the magical world. Hagrid's abrupt arrival at 'The-Hut-On-The-Rocks, The Sea' to claim Harry for Hogwarts at the beginning of *Harry Potter and the Philosopher's Stone* and the unwelcome sight of the Weasley brothers hovering in a flying car outside Harry's bedroom window in *Harry Potter and the Chamber of Secrets* are their only direct contact with someone from the other world.

In *Harry Potter and the Goblet of Fire*, the status of Harry's wizarding life is changed. He no longer flees into the night but is to be fetched by the Weasleys in an apparently normal, social visiting manner. But this intrusion of magic into the everyday lacks the transitional integrity of his previous journeys and the absence of any defined barrier reduces the impact of the differences between the two lives that Harry leads.

Floo powder, the magical dust which enables those of the wizarding world to travel freely through a network of chimneys, works relatively well while the Weasleys introduce Harry to transport within the magical world, from their own home to the wizarding shopping mall Diagon Alley, in *Harry Potter and the Chamber of Secrets*. It works much less well when the Weasleys arrive at the Dursleys' to take Harry home to go to the Quidditch World Cup in *Harry Potter and the Goblet of Fire*. Justified logistically by Mr Weasley announcing that he has added 4 Privet Drive to the Floo network, it still makes for an uncomfortable farce as wizards and

Muggles confront each other. The whirlwind of chaos the Weasleys cause in the Dursleys' sitting room is symbolic of this ill-defined barrier. Lacking the logic or precision of the train, the encounter becomes one of slapstick and comedy rather than magical invention.

In *Harry Potter and the Goblet of Fire*, Rowling is far more ambitious in scope than in the three previous titles. She adds a flurry of cross-overs between the worlds with varying success. The more clearly defined the separation, the more successful the travel that makes it possible. Least successful, partly because the nature of the world in which the Weasleys' home exists is never clearly defined, are the Portkeys by which the thousands of wizards reach the Quidditch World Cup. Designed not to draw attention to themselves within the Muggle world, they take the form of an insignificant object such as the old boot left on Stoatshead Hill which is the one the Weasleys, Harry and Hermione use.

With no obvious vehicle in which to make the journey, this form of collective travel depends wholly on a simplistic act of disappearance. Joining hands and holding the old boot on Mr Weasley's count of three, Harry feels a jerk just behind his navel and then nothing until his feet slam the ground. Like Floo powder, this lacks any basis in a recognizable reality and therefore does not have the charm of other magical methods of movement. But Rowling has created the Portkey for a far greater purpose and by establishing it as an apparently familiar means of getting about she can use it with conviction where it is really needed. Harry travels on a quite different journey the next time he, unwittingly, touches a Portkey. Again, after the count of three, Harry feels a jerk just below his navel as he and Cedric, choosing to share the winning honours between them, both grasp a handle of the Triwizard Cup. This time, when Harry feels his feet slamming into the ground, he is nowhere he has ever been before – and face to face with Voldemort. Despite taking off from a place in the real world when used to transport wizards to the Quidditch World Cup, the Portkey also links wizards within their own world.

Alongside the mass movement of the Weasley family and others by Portkey, the magical experience for individuals of 'Apparating' or 'Disapparating' is both much simpler and much subtler, partly because inherent within it is the idea that it is something you can only do when you are seventeen and when you've passed a test – a typical Rowling version of the familiar driving test which offers older teenagers exactly the same freedom of being able to travel on their own. Rowling's ease with this kind of magical variation and the way she weaves it into the fabric of an alternative world is reflected in the additional details about what can go wrong. In *Harry Potter and the Goblet of Fire* Mr Weasley tells a brief story of a young couple who Apparated without first passing the test and getting a licence – and with the disastrous result of 'splinching' themselves.

Rowling's linguistic humour is evident here and in her account she establishes a method of magical moving that has previously been mentioned but never defined. This is one of the many examples of Rowling fleshing out or embellishing ideas from one book to another. In discussion of how Sirius Black has broken into Hogwarts in *Harry Potter and the Prisoner of Azkaban*, Hermione, who has the information from her frequent reading of *Hogwarts, A History*, scoffs at the suggestion that he might have got past the Dementors either in disguise, or by knowing how to Apparate. She points out that the castle is protected by enchantments as well as walls and these stop people entering in irregular ways – such as Apparating. As ever, good rules enhance the power of the magic and Rowling is careful to ensure it does not become random or arbitrary.

Rowling uses the separation of time only once in the four books, in *Harry Potter and the Prisoner of Azkaban*. As a device, it is useful for allowing people to operate in worlds separated by time instead of place. As with the Portkeys, Rowling sets her time-shift carefully. Hermione is given a Time-Turner by the Ministry of Magic on Professor McGonagall's undertaking that she will use it only for her studies. It enables her to take a double timetable fitting in Muggle Studies and Divination as well as all her other subjects, a ploy wholly in keeping with her swotty inclinations. This worthy but somehow deplorable trick establishes limited time-travel as a gimmick that can be used for pedestrian purposes. Once established, it then serves an invaluable purpose in the same book when Hermione, as instructed by Dumbledore, hangs the magical hourglass around Harry's neck too, and he feels that he is flying backwards very fast. Together, Harry and Hermione relive their past three hours and so enable the story to be rewritten: for Buckbeak to escape from the executioner and Sirius Black and Buckbeak to fly away from the castle and their pursuers. More important, it allows Harry to understand that the strong Patronus which drives the Dementors from him is not created by his father but by himself. Rowling's careful control of this time-shift is well demonstrated by her intelligently conceived and executed construction.

CHAPTER 6

Society

The conventionality and old-fashioned nature of the boarding-school setting provides a framework for a series which reflects a similar morality. Though Rowling and her stories of Harry Potter have been condemned for encouraging an unhealthy interest in witches and witchcraft by members of some Fundamentalist religious sects in the US and have even been banned by one Church-of-England primary school in the United Kingdom for the same reason, the truth is very different. Rowling has written a series that is deeply humane, with real warmth towards all people; one that is based on the most conventional morality. While she subverts the external details of life, she has a clearly defined moral code which in the domestic context upholds family values – the large, loving Weasley family is well brought up, with children obeying parents on matters of importance, though sufficiently full of spirit and prankish to be fun; and social values, with rules and hierarchies based on order and control.

Rowling makes her points about society's values strongly. As with many other major fantasies such as C. S. Lewis's Narnia stories, Susan Cooper's *The Dark is Rising* quintet (1965–77), Alan Garner's *Elidor* (1965) or more recently Philip Pullman's *His Dark Materials* trilogy (1995–2000), the struggle is between opposing forces of good and evil. While Harry is the representative of the forces of enlightenment, Voldemort represents a dark world of torture, particularly mental torture, and oppression.

Late twentieth-century children's books encompass a wide range of genres, the most dominant of which is social realism. Rowling's Harry Potter, standing so firmly within the two most traditional conventions for children's books – school story and fantasy – seems an unlikely source of powerful story-telling about contemporary mores. And yet the underlying strand of all four novels, and it's a theme that is building through the series, is the destructive nature of racial discrimination. Through this, Rowling taps into one of the most important social issues of the time: the frightening recurrence of widespread ethnic cleansing, where hitherto harmonious peoples are violently divided, and minorities are systematically killed or driven out under the auspices of religion or ethnicity.

While political barriers are being broken down and geographical frontiers crossed with increasing ease and frequency, racial intolerance appears to be on the increase. In Britain, racially motivated incidents are widespread. Problems lie within communities where groups from different cultures clash and are also endemic within institutions which have allowed prejudice to pervade the structure.

Writing for children has always played a part in identifying real aspects of society as well as constructing imaginary worlds. Since the mid-1970s particularly, many children's writers have been vigorous in making sure the current social and political issues are familiar and intelligible to children. The divided society in Northern Ireland and how it affects children growing up there was sympathetically portrayed in Joan Lingard's *The Twelfth Day of July* (1970) and its sequels. Beverley Naidoo's *Journey to Jo'Burg* (1985) revealed the realities of apartheid for children growing up in South Africa. Most recently, three books within one year exposed the diverse problems of racial prejudice in contemporary Britain as seen from both the incomers' and the residents' perspectives. Bernard Ashley's *Little Soldier* (1999) follows the adjustments which a boy soldier brought to safety in Britain from the war in Uganda has to make, including finding himself in a class at school with a boy from the very tribe who killed his parents. Gaye Hicylmaz's *Girl in Red* (2000) touches on reactions to Eastern European gypsies arriving in Britain. Beverley Naidoo's *The Other Side of Truth* (2000) tells of the struggle for survival of two Nigerian children sent to safety in Britain after their mother is shot in front of them in Lagos, a reprisal for their father's outspoken journalism. All of these reflect the different aspects of immigration and attitudes to incomers which surround contemporary children.

With mass communications, children around the world are all too aware of the mental and physical cruelty which intolerance creates and they are disturbed by it. In reality they are unable to help but, within the fantasy world as Rowling has created it, it is the children themselves, guided by sympathetic adults, who are able to take a practical as well as a moral stance. In this, Rowling fulfils one of the key functions of fantasy which is to enable children to achieve beyond their capabilities; to act heroically and to take on adult responsibilities. From her very different starting point, Rowling confronts many of the same issues as the social realists. Including this serious background adds a dimension to the stories that gives them a relevance the purely magical themes lack.

Within the selective starting point, that pupils are chosen to attend Hogwarts, Rowling pursues the idea of differences of class and race. Wizard hierarchies are based on many things, including age, wealth and intelligence, but the central issue for the fanatics is one of purity of breeding. Within the parallel worlds of Wizards and Muggles there is a fair amount of cross-over, including inter-marriage. The theme of the importance of pure blood is one that Rowling is developing with the series, though the basis of it is already well established in *Harry Potter and the Philosopher's Stone*. The immediate enmity that springs up between Harry and Malfoy has much to do with Malfoy's ingrained attitude to pure blood which he alludes to at their very first meeting in Diagon Alley.

Malfoy is being fitted up for his uniform in *Madam Malkin's Robes for All Occasions* while his parents are buying other Hogwarts necessities. Hagrid has gone to the Leaky Cauldron for a pick-me-up, so Harry is alone. Wanting to place him socially, Malfoy first asks where Harry's parents are and then, on hearing that they are dead, he presses on with little sign of sympathy to find out whether they were of pure blood. Once Harry has confirmed that they were a witch and a wizard, Malfoy then establishes his own prejudiced position against the admitting of 'the other sort' into Hogwarts, mockingly saying that some have never even heard of the school before getting the letter. Since Harry, though of (mostly) pure blood, had heard about his place at Hogwarts in exactly the way Malfoy has just ridiculed, there is an obvious hostility between the two boys despite the fact that both belong to wizarding families.

Malfoy reveals further layers of prejudice in his hierarchical view of society on their second meeting on the Hogwarts Express when he finds Harry with Ron and advises him to keep better company. He dismisses the Weasleys not for their lack of breeding – they are as pure blood as the Malfoys – but for their lack of money. He hopes to enlist Harry into his camp by sneering at Ron. Harry's immediate rejection of Malfoy's offer and his confidence in proclaiming his ability to make his own judgements of who are the wrong sort heightens the tension between the two. It leads Malfoy to threaten Harry with the fate of his parents, incidentally revealing something of the background to Harry's inheritance. Through these two encounters Rowling establishes Harry as liberal on issues of class and race.

An old wizarding family, the Malfoys are obsessed with true blood and old-fashioned rules of wizard behaviour. They have all the trappings of the establishment: visible wealth, servants and local power. This social status protects them from open accusations of links with Voldemort although there is an implicit understanding that such links exist. Rowling signals her disapproval of such people in many ways apart from their evident connections with the powers of darkness. When Harry makes a mistake on his first attempt at using Floo powder in *Harry Potter and the Chamber of Secrets*, he ends up in Knockturn Alley, the sinister neighbouring street to Diagon Alley. Here he overhears Malfoy's father Lucius conducting some shady business with the obsequious Mr Borgin, disposing of some dubious goods which might prove to be an embarrassment if discovered under the newly proposed Muggle Protection Act. Rowling immediately equates wealth and power with the possibility – or even probability – of corruption.

In contrast, Harry has unique status within the wizarding world. He does have Muggle blood since his mother was not born into a wizarding family (hence having Aunt Petunia for a sister) but his defeat of Voldemort marks him out as someone who has a destiny which puts him outside the normal social structure. His lack of wizarding knowledge, which would be a distinct social disadvantage for others coming to Hogwarts, is seen as quite acceptable in his case.

Armed with this, Harry is able to cross all the complex social or racial barriers that are threaded through the wizarding world. He is able to act as a conduit for Rowling's ideas of an inclusive society. Because of his isolated childhood, he is unfamiliar with the concepts of 'pure blood' and the derogatory 'mud blood' which defines those from mixed or non-wizard marriages. Through his choice of friends, Ron and Hermione, he shows that he takes a stand for toleration on matters of birth and social status. Ron, though from an unimpeach-able Wizarding family, is poor; Hermione, though the best student of her year, is a first-generation wizard – her parents are dentists in the Muggle world. She makes up for her lack of breeding through the power of knowledge (a familiar device in socially divisive societies): she keeps herself better informed than the pure bloods and so has important views to add. Between the three of them, they represent a wide spectrum of types of wizards in terms of birth and wealth, and challenge the orthodoxy that an inherited place in society is superior.

Rowling touches on this theme of social or racial status as she introduces Harry's Hogwarts contemporaries. Neville Longbottom, though himself an inadequate Wizard with a terrible reputation for forgetfulness, comes from a distinguished family. His parents are out of the picture – the exact circumstances of their absence is only revealed in *Harry Potter and the Goblet of Fire* when Professor Moody demonstrates the Cruciatus curse, the hideous torture which reduced Neville's parents to insanity and led to their incarceration in St Mungo's Hospital for Magical Maladies and Injuries. In their place, Neville has been brought up by his grandmother, a witch with a considerable reputation: what he lacks in his skills is more than compensated for by his breeding. Seamus Finnegan has a Muggle father and witch mother and quite enough confidence to fight the corner of the half-blood (plus some stereotypical Irish charm), while Justin Finch-Fletchley proclaims his social status in Muggle terms by revealing that he would have gone to Eton had he not suddenly been selected for Hogwarts. It's an admission that makes him vulnerable when the attacks on the Hogwarts pupils begin in *Harry Potter and the Chamber of Secrets*. In a nod, though not much more, Rowling also creates a community that would appear to be mixed in the real world with the inclusion of the Patil twins, Cho Chang, Angelina Johnson and Lee Jordan with his dreadlocks.

The clearly differentiated characteristics of each of the houses create another social order of a determinist nature. Families tend, though there are exceptions, to belong to the same house down through generations so the particular qualities of each, as defined by the Sorting Hat at the beginning of Harry's first year, apply to birth and background as much as to the current individual. As defined by the school song, Hufflepuffs are patient, loyal and hardworking, Ravenclaws are brainy, Gryffindors are courageous and chivalrous while Slytherins are cunning and ruthless.

With Harry, his parents, Dumbledore and Sirius Black as Gryffindors and Voldemort, Malfoy and his parents, and Professor Snape as Slytherins there are clear demarcations laid down. As each pupil is allocated to a particular house on first arrival at Hogwarts, Rowling to some extent contradicts her open-mindedness to their destiny.

Social and racial credentials are established in *Harry Potter and the Philosopher's Stone* showing them to be an important underpinning of the whole framework though they only play a small part in the story. Different reactions to them, and especially Harry's own, provide an underlying morality and perspective. Issues of racial purity and wealth and class occur time and again throughout the four titles and tie in closely with the struggle between good and evil as embodied by Harry and Voldemort. There is a clear link, which develops throughout the series, between those who are racially prejudiced and those who are followers of Voldemort, the 'Dark Lord', part of whose darkness is a hatred of Muggles and those who, like himself, are of mixed blood, a hatred that is fuelled by his Muggle father's rejection of his witch mother before he was born and his subsequent upbringing in a Muggle orphanage.

Rowling is secure in her treatment of this social structure, and her ability directly and through sharp satire to sustain the arguments about it is one of the greatest strengths of the first three books. By making inclusion into the wizarding world dependent on aptitude for magic as well as on birth she deliberately creates a mixed community which includes different social hierarchies.

Through her descriptions of them she creates clear guidelines in her social commentary without preaching. These add to the substance of the books, taking them beyond the simple struggle between good and evil or the fun of a wizarding boarding school where unlikely things might happen.

Exchanges around purity of race remain relatively discreet in *Harry Potter and the Philosopher's Stone* in that they are stated but not further pursued and the theme is explored tangentially to the central plot. It becomes critical to the plot in *Harry Potter and the Chamber of Secrets* and shapes the build up to the ultimate confrontation which, as in all four titles, is between Voldemort or his supporters and Harry. When the Chamber of Secrets is opened, all the attacks are on those who are not of pure blood. Last opened fifty years before, the Chamber of Secrets can only be opened by the powers of Salazar Slytherin and his heirs, all of whom regard themselves as pure blood. Suspicion falls on Harry as the person who has petrified the victims when it is discovered he can speak the snake language of Parseltongue. But when the truth is revealed, it is the memory of Voldemort, in the form of the diary of his childhood identity Tom Riddle, which has insidiously manipulated Ginny Weasley to open the Chamber.

The rise in importance of the conflict between the pure bloods and the rest is highlighted by the far more explosive exchanges in the second book. As ever, Harry's ignorance of the language and ways of the wizarding world act is used to good effect. Harry has to ask for simple information and clarification which informs the reader too. Though he is not familiar with the word Malfoy uses when he calls Hermione a 'filthy little Mudblood' he knows from the response of the crowd and Ron in particular, who performs a curse that backfires, that some line of decorum has been overstepped.

Explanation for Harry, Hermione (who as a Mudblood is not expected to know) and readers comes from Ron as he recovers from his backfired curse which makes him belch up slugs. He explains the offensive nature of the name calling and then, supported by Hagrid, points out that pure-blood wizards may be useless – as with Neville whose spells invariably go wrong – and equally that Muggle-born witches and wizards may have superior talents, Hermione being an obvious example. Ron also points out that marriage between wizards and Muggles has always been a necessity to prevent the wizarding world from dying out.

With this exchange and explanation, the battle lines between the two sides are laid out and new characters such as Colin Creevey are given a position on one or other side of the divide, positions which are easily readable by which house additional characters are put into and whether they become acolytes of Malfoy or acquaintances of Harry, Ron and Hermione. The centrality of the disagreement and the mounting anger and then physical danger which it generates makes *Harry Potter and the Chamber of Secrets* a much more intense and dramatic book then *Harry Potter and the Philosopher's Stone*.

The petrification of the Mudbloods has sinister overtones. The idea that some individuals are being picked off in what initially seem like unrelated attacks is very scary to an enclosed community. When they discover the link between the victims, it is even more horrific. Rowling's ability to build tension makes it a convincing parallel to the persecution of any minority within a society.

With *Harry Potter and the Prisoner of Azkaban*, Rowling takes off in a different direction concentrating largely on inner fears and questions about the loyalty of friends, though the animosities are still there and the issue of pure bloods as opposed to the other wizards has not totally disappeared. But, in *Harry Potter and the Goblet of Fire*, behind the struggle between Harry and Voldmort she returns almost exclusively to different aspects of racism. Using the framework of the Quidditch World Cup and then the Triwizard Tournament as devices to get wizards from other countries together, thus adding an international element, she expands the theme of tolerance into considerations of nationalism as well as racism. It is a theme best summed up by Dumbeldore at the Leaving Feast at the end of the book in which he says that friendship, trust and common aims can overcome differences in culture and language. He urges all to unite in order to confront the discord that Voldemort is trying to spread.

The inclusion of an international element reflects a far more ambitious scope for Rowling. The addition of an enormous new cast drawn from all over the world enables her to bring in a new and particularly sinister version of the kind of arguments Ron and Harry have been having with Malfoy. The hooded gang which first persecutes Muggles by humiliating and teasing them and is then associated with the raising of the Dark Mark is closely modelled on the Ku Klux Klan in the southern states of the US.

In this outdoor setting, far away from the comparatively tame and rule-bound fantasy world of Hogwarts, prejudice turns into hatred and is suddenly far more sinister, fitting with the generally more chilling and deeper evil as Voldemort becomes ever more potent. Here Rowling is consistent with all that has gone before: the stakes are raised and the tension mounts. Mob rule is as unpleasant here as it is anywhere in the 'real' world.

But the representation of the different countries that Rowling presents, both with the stereotypes of the two teams taking part in the Quidditch World Cup and later on with the arrival at Hogwarts of the two wizarding schools to compete for the Triwizard Tournament, is far harder to handle. The difference lies in the fact that the divisions and tensions within the wizarding world are imitations of the class, money and power divisions that lie within any society. As with much else, Rowling adapts and mimics, making localized prejudices which are both instantly recognizable and original. When Mr and Mrs Malfoy spot almost the entire Weasley family in the top box at the Quidditch match, Mr Malfoy cannot resist sneering about the relative values of the Weasleys' home and the cost of the seats – a cheap jibe which could be used in any social context.

Defining people by nationality depends largely on using the best-known, and therefore the most stereotypical characteristics. Though clearly intended as parody, the two competing teams at the Quidditch World Cup – Bulgaria and Ireland – are defined by simplistic, nationalist emblems and mascots. Irish jokes abound: the shimmering shamrock which precedes the team into the stadium erupts into thousands of leprechauns – little bearded men in green, the colour traditionally associated with Ireland. The Bulgarian team has the sexy, Siren-like Veelas as its mascot and a Minister for Magic whom Mr Fudge first insults by making a joke out of his name and then dismisses by pointing out that he can't speak any English anyway so that such rudeness doesn't matter. Europeans with thick, foreign accents are to be laughed at and Irish blarney indulged: it is harmless fun but, given the strength of Rowling's previously inclusive attitude, it certainly comes as a surprise. However, the foreigners do get the last laugh as the leprechaun gold turns to dust and the Bulgarian Minister for Magic turns out to be fluent in English.

The same problems beset the descriptions of the members of the two schools travelling to Hogwarts with their champions for the Triwizard Tournament. Beauxbatons from France and Durmstrang from Eastern Europe are full of nationalistic characteristics, apparently evident in the sent-up versions of their appearance and speech. When greeted by Professor Dumbledore as she steps down from the Beauxbatons carriage, Madame Maxime breaks into charmingly broken English – including a very over-Frenchified version of Dumbledore's name which she delivers in a deep voice with a clearly implied undercurrent of sexuality. Her later exchanges, such as when she remonstrates that Hogwarts has an extra champion for the Triwizard Tournament, are delivered in equally stereotypical fractured English. The only other significant character from Beauxbatons, its champion Fleur Delacour, is a beautiful girl with a sheet of silvery blonde hair. The French are encapsulated as both charming in their manners and physically attractive.

In contrast, Karkaroff the head of Durmstrang is portrayed as physically unattractive with implications that he is dishonest. With a weak chin and a smile that doesn't reach his eyes, he is at worst calculating and at best unctuous. His champion, Viktor Krum, the star of the Bulgarian Quidditch team, fares better though he is also frequently described as 'surly'. Idolized by the boys for his sporting prowess he is also searched out by the girls who mob him in the library. But Durmstrang is definitely suspect from the beginning – mention by Malfoy that he might have been sent there because they practise the Dark Arts confirms this – and their ship moored on the Hogwart's lake is dark and foreboding while the Beauxbatons' powder-blue carriage is well lit and appealing. The Durmstrang students are immediately more sinister and the subsequent discovery that Karkaroff was once a Death Eater endorses the idea that these people, who have only thinly disguised Germanic characteristics, are both nationally and individually untrustworthy.

Jokes at the foreigners' expense continue: at dinner Ron points out a large shellfish stew on offer beside the equally symbolic steak-and-kidney pudding. Immediately suspicious he asks Hermione what it is. Her answer, 'Bouillabaisse', he then pretends to mishear as a sneeze and says, 'Bless you' – an old school-story joke from an era when making jokes about foreign words or names was acceptable.

Even Dumbledore seems to fall into the trap of making a nationalist joke – a wizard's equivalent of a Scotsman, an Irishman and an Englishman – when he launches into a story about a troll, a hag and a leprechaun who all go into a bar. Fortunately, Professor McGonagall has the good sense to stop him before he gets too carried away.

But equality between nations is not the only social theme that Rowling tackles in *Harry Potter and the Goblet of Fire*. Having given up her enriched time-table, Hermione adopts the cause of the House Elves. She carries out her campaign to free them with very little support, even from Harry and Ron. Ron adopts the line that elves enjoy working for other people and even Harry, whose instincts are usually so sure and who has so confidently and determinedly freed Dobby from his enslavement to the Malfoys, is equivocal about becoming too involved in Hermione's Society for the Promotion of Elfish Welfare (SPEW), or House-Elf Liberation Front as it becomes known. The elves themselves as represented by Dobby and Winky, two of Rowling's most endearing characters largely on account of their inflected speech which imbues them with a delightful immaturity, confuse matters further by not knowing what they want out of freedom or, in the case of Winky who takes to the bottle once released from serving the Crouch family, whether they want it at all. Rowling is thoughtful about the differences between paid service and personal service, which Hermione rightly sees as slavery, and the difficulty of adapting to independence. The house elves, like servants or slaves in any other society, are also keepers of family secrets and Winky's revelations about the goings-on in the Crouch household are critical to unravelling the background to the Triwizard Tournament and Harry's near-fatal encounter with Voldemort.

Hermione's obsessive adoption of the cause, and her total lack of insight into just how boring she is being about it, is a brief episode within *Harry Potter and the Goblet of Fire* and one which Rowling allows to peter out without complete resolution. But within it lies yet another example of Rowling's ability to create her own version of someone familiar by touching on all the identifying hallmarks of campaign leaders: tunnel vision, bullying tactics to get others involved and, sometimes, a persistence in pursuing a course of action which may look as if it lies against the best interests of those it is aiming to help.

Rowling's commitment to issues of equality and her contempt for prejudice provide both a social framework and a moral background which underpin the adventures that propel the narrative of the stories. Her instinctive support for the underdog – on an individual basis as with orphaned Harry and on a societal basis as with the house elves – is part of the reason children identify with the stories as strongly as they do. Children themselves are relatively powerless within society and so are quick to recognize empathy for others in the same or similar situations.

The differences of race and wealth are overtly discussed among the pupils of Hogwarts and Rowling repeatedly attempts to portray an inclusive society founded on equality. Gender differences – or similarities – are not so openly discussed and Rowling appears to contradict her own view of a modern society by giving mixed messages about the status of girls and women in her magical world.

In terms of structure, everything at Hogwarts appears to be meted out fairly. It is a mixed school, the boys and girls study the same curriculum and, as far as the clothes are described – work robes, a pointed hat, gloves and a cloak – their uniforms are identical. They share lessons and sit together at meals, only having separate sleeping and bathroom arrangements. All play Quidditch in mixed teams, though the Gryffindor captain Wood, in what seems like an expectation of male membership, does make the mistake of addressing the team as 'men' in his pre-match pep talk before he is corrected by Angelina Johnson, the team Chaser.

The staff, too, is completely mixed and the teachers are not, for the most part, stereotypically divided by the subjects they teach, though there are some obvious lapses such as the unfortunately caricatured draconian librarian, Madam Pince. Madam Hooch, for example, is the sports teacher and chief Quidditch coach and, while Dumbledore rules supreme as headmaster, Professor McGonagall runs the day-to-day affairs of Hogwarts and maintains the necessary order as well as being an imposing and clever teacher of Transfiguration which includes some of the most complex and dangerous magic taught at Hogwarts. But the roles of headteacher and deputy are not a defined sexual hierarchy as is shown when the Beauxbatons pupils appear in *Harry Potter and the Goblet of Fire*, led by their statuesque headmistress, Madame Maxime who is herself a redoubtable witch with considerable powers. Even in its history, Hogwarts is shown to be non-sexist having great female witches as well as great wizards among its founders. Of the four school houses, two were founded by women and two by men. This sound principle is marginally undermined by the fact that Slytherin and Gryffindor, which are undoubtedly the two dominant houses, were founded by men while Ravenclaw and Hufflepuff, described respectively as for those of ready mind and those who are patient and true, were founded by women.

From these beginnings, Rowling creates a school which appears to value the genders equally and to develop their talents without differentiation between the sexes. When it comes to choosing a champion for the Triwizard Tournament in *Harry Potter and the Goblet of Fire* the barrier is age not sex. Angelina Johnson from Gryffindor is one of the first to enter her name and when the final list of champions is called, Fleur Delacour from Beauxbatons is chosen. In the subsequent trials, which are as much about intelligence as strength, there is no suggestion that she is any less able than the boys to compete effectively. In smaller tests of bravery, and magical tasks in class, girls are also perfectly capable of performing all the same skills as the boys. In Professor Lupin's revealing lessons on Boggarts in *Harry Potter and the Prisoner of Azkaban* there is even a mild sexist inversion as Parvati conjures up the Boggart as a mummy while Ron, whose greatest fear is spiders, faces up to and defeats one.

Structurally, therefore, Hogwarts allows for equality and Rowling gives every impression that that is her intention. It would certainly be in keeping with the other values she conveys. However, throughout all four books she is overtly or implicitly negative about her female characters giving them at best limited and at worst demeaning roles.

In her descriptions of the pupils, Rowling is distinctly sparing in her characterization of the girls, in their development and in the roles she gives them. Hermione is the only identifiable girl pupil in *Harry Potter and the Philosopher's Stone*. Here, she is an excellent foil to Harry and her intelligence plays a vital part in fulfilling the missions which Harry and Ron undertake. She is sensible without being prim and her cleverness is appreciated. Hermione is interesting, amusing and valuable.

Surprisingly, Rowling develops her role in subsequent titles by adding less positive sides to her character. In a stereotype of swatty girls, Hermione becomes something of a blue-stocking bore – a position that is confirmed by the double timetable she adopts in *Harry Potter and the Prisoner of Azkaban*. Worse befalls her in *Harry Potter and the Goblet of Fire* when she is recast as a passionate do-gooder, so committed to the cause of freeing house elves that she becomes a crusading zealot. These developments undermine the more positive aspects of her continuing commitment to supporting Harry, the value of her knowledge, perceptiveness and initiative, and her surprise emergence as Viktor Krum's charming and striking partner at the Yule Ball.

Other girls fare even less well. There is little mention of them in lessons except for Lavender and Parvati who are much-mocked by Harry and Ron for their credulity in Professor Trelawney's Divination lessons and whose contribution to the Care of Magical Creatures classes, whether with Hagrid and his assorted monsters or with Professor Grubbly-Plank and her beautiful unicorn, is limited to squeals of Oooooooh! Ginny Weasley plays a significant part in *Harry Potter and the Chamber of Secrets* – mostly because she needs to be rescued – but she is largely defined by her devotion to Harry; she blushes scarlet every time he appears and is rendered speechless in his presence. Cho Chan, a girl in the year above to whom Harry is attracted, is without substance except that she is pretty, though she does also pass a kind word to Harry when everything seems at its bleakest. Angelina Johnson, a feisty black girl, is largely noted for her prowess in Quidditch.

Even the old girls of Hogwarts fare badly. Bertha Jorkins, Percy Weasley's colleague in the Ministry of Magic and the only female professional in the outside world, is written off as hopeless by Percy and even by the Hogwarts teachers. Their assessments prove correct when she turns out to have fallen into Voldemort's power and to have given him essential information under torture before being killed by him.

Only Fleur Delacour, the Beauxbatons champion whose selection causes the other Beauxbatons hopefuls to cry, has a sustained and fulfilling role while also revealing entirely convincing emotions, such as her genuine distress when she thinks she has failed to rescue her sister from the Grindylows.

Feminine emotions, camaraderie and mutual support between the girls – or even petty enmities and squabbles – all of which might be expected in an enclosed community such as Hogwarts, are missing. While Harry and Ron have a relationship that develops, including in *Harry Potter and the Goblet of Fire* surviving Ron's growing jealousy of Harry's fame, wealth and success, the girls and their relationships remain dormant. The only signs of their development and presumed maturity are their interest in having the right partner for the Yule Ball. Though another example of somewhat diminished roles,

Rowling uses it to produce a moment of wit, as Harry and Ron completely fail to find partners, largely because of their inability to see Hermione as an attractive girl whom they might invite.

If the girls in the school are largely just ignored, Rowling is positively pejorative in her descriptions of almost all the other females within Hogwarts. The character in the picture which guards the Gryffindor tower is the Fat Lady; her friend, who pops out of her picture in the ante room to the great hall and brings the surprising news of the extra Triwizard champion, is called Violet but is referred to as the Wizened Witch. Both are defined as physically unattractive by their names and contrast with the unreliable but engaging Sir Cadogan who takes a turn as stand-in when the Fat Lady gets damaged. The ghost who haunts the girls' bathroom so spectacularly in *Harry Potter and the Chamber of Secrets* is Moaning Myrtle; like the portraits she is immediately a character to be despised while her male counterpart in the ghost world, Nearly Headless Nick, is a charming if hopeless figure of fun. Only Mrs Norris, the caretaker's disagreeable female cat, is matched by an equally disagreeable male counterpart, Mr Filch himself.

Outside Hogwarts in the village of Hogsmeade, Madam Rosmerta, the barmaid serving foaming tankards of Butterbeer at the Three Broomsticks, is described from a male perspective with the implication that she is easy on the eye and, as such, very much part of the charm of being in the Three Broomsticks in the first place. Even Rita Skeeter, one of Rowling's greatest comic creations with her cheap journalism made all the easier with her Quick-Quotes Quill, is yet another unfavourable female stereotype.

Within the two main families in both the non-magical and the magical world, women, whether the vile Aunt Petunia or the adored Mrs Weasley, spend most of their time sorting out petty domestic matters. Both produce the correct school uniforms for their children – multiplied many times over in Mrs Weasley's case – and both cook for their respective families. Mrs Weasley rustles up enormous meals, though luckily she does have some magical help for chopping up potatoes and making sauces when she has all of her family and Harry and Hermione staying. Other kinds of mothers, such as Draco Malfoy's glamorous but sneering mother who appears briefly at the World Quidditch Cup, are clearly despised. Blonde, slim and potentially nice-looking, Mrs Malfoy is called Narcissa.

Even in the world of the non-wizards, among the elves released from their house servitude, Dobby manages his freedom intelligently by finding himself a job and assuming some self-respect. Winky, however, takes to drink and falls into a stupor of self-pity, begging to be allowed to revert to her slavery.

Rowling, who has such a clear understanding of the need for equality and tolerance in society, and who starts out with good role models of female teachers, surprises in the overall female role models that she has created. While her girl characters are capable of being intelligent and competent, they appear naturally to adopt subservient or stereotypical roles. In this, Rowling reverts to the patterns of children's books before the mid-1950s which, with a few exceptions, invariably cast girls as either practical or sensitive, as Susan and Titty are in Arthur Ransome's *Swallows and Amazons* (1930), or as Susan and Lucy are in C.S. Lewis's Narnia sequence. Rarely were girls given leading roles in stories with characters of both sexes, though there are many characterful and determined girls from the period such as Pippi in Astrid Lingren's *Pippi Longstocking* (1946), first published in the UK in 1954, or Dorothy Edwards's life-affirming *My Naughty Little Sister* (1954) for younger readers.

Though Rowling gives Hermione many of the same attributes, she has not developed her role in a way which matches the model of girls who prevailed in the post-war decades: heroines such as Marie in Gillian Avery's *The Warden's Niece* (1957), Dido Twite in Joan Aiken's *Black Hearts in Battersea* (1964), Jessica Vye in Jane Gardam's *A Long Way from Verona* (1971), Carrie in Nina Bawden's *Carrie's War* (1973), Madge in Jill Paton Walsh's *Goldengrove* (1973), and there are many more. These girls were filled with self-doubts and confusion, and often appeared shy, but were also resourceful leaders, humorous and capable of adapting themselves to situations, or situations to themselves.

In this, Rowling may have been influenced by the current publishing orthodoxy that boys do not read and certainly do not read about girls, which is why Harry is such a dominant character. If this is so, she has been entirely successful since Harry Potter appears to be as popular with girls as with boys. While boy readers may identify with Harry's heroism, girl readers, like the girls at Hogwarts, respond to him both as a motherless boy in need of love and as a romantic hero with special powers.

As the books become increasingly dramatic and the dangers which Harry faces escalate, his role as romantic hero is growing. In *Harry Potter and the Philosopher's Stone*, the search for the Philosopher's Stone is a small part of the drama. Harry's origins and establishing the Hogwarts background are the core to the book's identity. When Harry, Hermione and Ron set out to discover the Philosopher's

Stone and in so doing unmask Quirrell and reveal Voldemort, it is little more than an 'after lights-out' adventure that grows with the addition of some highly dramatic magical moments.

As the series progresses, Harry is less and less of an ordinary child. His status marks him out for the roles that he takes on, making him part of legend rather than a schoolboy. In terms of telling, Rowling moves from school story to myth. In all the subsequent titles Harry is taken into Dumbledore's study. He is the Arthur to Dumbledore's Merlin. The battle between Voldemort and Harry is reset as part of an age-old magical mythology and, as such, the role of women is also altered so that they too, become part of the different literary tradition.

CHAPTER 7

Education

While Rowling is broadly liberal in her view of society she is far more conformist in her view of education. Part of the innate conservatism of the stories is their old-fashioned setting. But Rowling's conventionality goes well beyond the mere setting of Hogwarts or the creation of a boarding school. Within the stories, Rowling's educational structure, content and assessment are all designed to shore up a very traditional kind of education, albeit with some jokey differences. The fact that the lessons are individually quirky gives scope for her tremendous imagination but it does not lessen the weight she attaches to the importance of formal teaching and learning. But Rowling saves her educational model from appearing entirely outdated by applying knowledge of the current educational system which enables her to make the parallel at Hogwarts a particularly telling and funny mirror of reality.

Addressed as Professor, Hogwarts teachers are invested with learning: they are, for the most part, respected by the pupils and they are certainly treated with the utmost courtesy. At meal times they sit at a high table, a place both of honour and remote from the pupils themselves. Their only regular contact with the pupils is as teachers not as carers. Even the heads of houses do not have any domestic interaction with the pupils, except if the pupils are in the Infirmary. Hogwarts pupils do not hurtle along corridors swinging their school bags; there is no shouting out in class – this is not a magical version of the contemporary comprehensive as it is currently shown in fiction. As in fictionalized public schools, control is maintained by the giving or taking away of house points and by the imposition of detentions. It is an order that is reinforced by the head boy and prefects, complete with badges and privileges. House points and detentions, though the pupils may think them unjustly awarded, represent a degree of order within a world of magical possibilities. All of these provide known boundaries and penalties which offer a kind of relief after the unknown risks that are thrown up by Harry's encounters with Voldemort. Through this juxtaposition Rowling endorses the value of structure and a rule-bound society. She applauds the formality of Hogwarts, emphasizing the safety and security which such an institution creates rather than identifying the repressive aspects that are the other side of the equation.

As with any school, much of the style and tone of Hogwarts comes from its head. Unlike so much of Hogwarts which lies in imitation and characterization, in Albus Dumbledore Rowling has created an original and complex headmaster. Firstly a magician, Dumbledore is also authoritative and headmasterly. He is as wise as his many years, not only in learning but also in humanity. His benign regime infuses Hogwarts with a background of warmth and decency which further accentuates school as a haven of personal growth and safety, despite the minor incidents of bullying.

Harry's first sight of Dumbledore comes from the Famous Witches and Wizards card he finds in his chocolate frogs packet on his first journey to Hogwarts. On the card, Dumbledore is described as considered by many the greatest wizard of modern times, thus confirming all that Hagrid has told Harry. When Harry first sees him in the flesh, Dumbledore's silver hair shines more brightly than anything in the hall except the ghosts. Dumbledore's authority is never in doubt. Yet he is also childlike or perhaps a bit 'mad' as Harry first thinks with the strange pronouncement of his four incon-sequential words, 'Nitwit! Blubber! Oddment! Tweak!', at the start of the feast in *Harry Potter and the Philosopher's Stone*.

Dumbledore is a protector. His care extends to all the pupils in the school but, most particularly, to Harry. His appearances at critical moments in Harry's life and his invitations to Harry to come into his study, an inner sanctuary which hardly anyone else except Hagrid enters, are indications of the special bond between the two.

Most specifically, his considerable powers enable him to keep the Dementors out of the school, despite the wishes of the Ministry of Magic which wants to employ them to find Sirius Black in *Harry*

Potter and the Prisoner of Azkaban. Dumbledore disapproves of the Dementors and despises their methods, seeing them as being too closely related to Voldemort and the powers of darkness. As a training ground for future practitioners of the skills of witchcraft and wizardry, Hogwarts is led by someone who has great powers of magic as well as the necessary headmasterly attributes of commanding authority. These come into effect when dealing with the issues within his own community, such as the appointment of staff, as well as having to attend meetings with the outside world, in his case the Ministry of Magic which ultimately controls the school.

Within the daily business of school, Dumbledore is a benign but distant figure who makes few appearances. The letter inviting Harry to Hogwarts comes from Professor McGonagall, not from Dumbledore, as if he is above the administration of the process of admissions. Yet, once he has reached Harry, Hagrid replies directly to Dumbledore, indicating the particular and special link not only between Harry and Dumbledore but also between Hagrid and Dumbledore. Discipline is controlled by the Heads of Houses; Dumbledore, who could have had a senior post in government, is set above such mundane wrangles. His appearances are bound up with breaches of a magical nature. It is Dumbledore who keeps the forces of darkness out of Hogwarts, though with the appointment of two out of the four Defence Against the Dark Arts teachers he mistakenly allows them into the school in the guises of Professor Quirrell in *Harry Potter and the Philosopher's Stone,* and the false Mad-Eye Moody in *Harry Potter and the Goblet of Fire* whose power is such that he manages to evade even Dumbledore's detection.

Professor Snape, unlike almost all the other characters in the Harry Potter books, occupies an interestingly ambiguous position and one that is changing as the series develops. A more powerful character than most of the Hogwarts teachers, his development is an example of Rowling's ability to change details while retaining the overall impression through the sequence of stories.

As head of Slytherin, Snape is immediately defined as 'cunning' in the words of the school song. Association with Slytherin means links, too, with Voldemort which marks Snape out as on the other side from Dumbledore, Harry and his parents. Within the contained and domestic situation of Hogwarts, Snape is in opposition to Harry in the giving out of house points when it comes to skirmishes between the Slytherins and the Gryffindors. But the enmity between Snape and Harry goes beyond simple house jealousies and divisions. Snape appears to hate Harry personally and by implication they are on opposing sides in the grander conflict between good and evil.

In her first description of him in *Harry Potter and the Philosopher's Stone*, Snape's physical characteristics of greasy dark hair, sallow skin and a hooked nose are an example of Rowling's sometimes clichéd use of expression which immediately casts Snape as a stereotyped villain. Snape's lessons take place in a dungeon, he is apparently always after the job of teacher of the Dark Arts and Harry's stab of pain in his scar on his first day at Hogwarts seems to come when the hook-nosed teacher looks past Professor Quirrell's turban straight at him. Throughout *Harry Potter and the Philosopher's Stone* and *Harry Potter and the Chamber of Secrets*, Snape is a suspicious character. Harry and his friends readily jump to the wrong conclusions when he's overheard getting Filch to bandage the wound on his leg and explaining the problem of keeping his eyes on all three heads of the monster guarding the Philosopher's Stone, which Harry interprets as meaning that he was trying to steal it, and in Harry's first Quidditch match when Snape is suspected of jinxing his broomstick.

Rowling is highly successful in both implicating Snape in dark moments while also making sure that the judgements and interpretations of those moments come from Harry and his friends, not from any of the adults in authority. Through his hatred of Snape, Harry works out much of his anger: for him, Snape represents an embodiment of Voldemort and, as such, is implicated in the death of James and Lily Potter. While superficially the relationship between Harry and Snape remains largely unchanged, the framework for it is completely altered by the revelations in *Harry Potter and the Prisoner of Azkaban* and *Harry Potter and the Goblet of Fire*. Snape's hatred of James Potter stems from when the latter saved his life after a schoolboy prank almost went disastrously wrong. It is a human hatred, stemming from schoolboy jealousy which he transfers to Harry. Also revealed is Snape's own past: once a Death Eater – and he still bears the mark – he has secretly changed sides which is why he is so trusted by Dumbeldore.

Snape's ambiguity and Rowling's skill in creating a character who both fascinates and remains convincing as he changes adds an engrossing element of surprise amidst the stability of Hogwarts which otherwise only changes with the arrival of new characters.

In Dumbledore and Snape, Rowling shows her ability to create original and rounded characters who, though cast in particular roles, have depth and substance which puts them beyond the positions which they represent. Superficially they fit into the traditions of the school story but Rowling has also bound them into the magical world of which Hogwarts is a central part.

As with much else in her writing, Rowling is particularly creative where she takes the germ of something familiar and turns it into something else. The best and most completely realized of the other Hogwarts teachers are recognizable take-offs of characters familiar in schools but, like the environment in which they teach, they are conventional stereotypes, not the more modern images of contemporary teachers. Professor Binns, the only ghost teacher on the staff, who teaches History of Magic – 'easily the most boring lesson' – remains shadowy throughout the series, though what he teaches proves useful to Hermione, and the history of the magical world which he imparts in his lessons is a convincing imitation of the kind of old-fashioned chronological history that was once taught in schools. Others, such as Professor Sprout, the Herbology teacher, are clearly established in *Harry Potter and the Philosopher's Stone* and are then developed throughout the series. Short and dumpy with dirty fingernails and an air of cheery obsession with the study of fungi and the outdoors, Professor Sprout is easily recognizable as the enthusiastic, slightly dotty biology teacher who expects everyone to be as interested in her subject as she is herself. Herbology lessons take place in the greenhouses just outside the school. This gives Professor Sprout a domain of her own in which to pursue her study of nature and her lessons include much potting of plants and dividing of roots. It is under her care that the wonderful growing of the mandrakes as a cure for the Petrification curse takes place in *Harry Potter and the Chamber of Secrets*. Rowling switches effortlessly from the traditional model she has created to an elaborate and well-constructed joke about how the mandrakes grow and develop, mirroring the stages of childhood and especially adolescence, drawing on and adapting the true information that mandrakes do look like curled-up babies. Real information and humour are easily intertwined in Rowling's invention.

In the delivering of the Hogwarts lessons Rowling is more up to date. Pupils are taught in small groups with lots of co-operative class work – practising spells in pairs in Snape's scary potions lessons, working in pairs or groups with Hagrid's often disgusting and sometimes dangerous animals in Care of Magical Creatures classes. In *Harry Potter and the Prisoner of Azkaban*, the curriculum is increased with the addition of new subjects after two years at the school and with the choice of different subjects – some softer options than others – very much in line with the contemporary school curriculum. It also allows for the introduction of new teachers, most notably the wonderfully mystical and wholly capricious Professor Trelawney, Harry's much-derided teacher of Divination. Talk of OWLs in the fifth year and NEWTs to follow – the two years of national tests – mirrors the assessments of GCSE and A levels.

Hogwarts pupils are set quantities of homework, some with despised specifications including filling a certain length of parchment, measured in feet and inches. Rowling's earnest and lofty tone on education is softened somewhat on the subject of homework but she never dismisses real learning lightly or underestimates its worth. Hermione's attitude is conveyed as rather over-conscientious and, though Ron and Harry are encouraged to work harder for some teachers, there is tacit support for their invented and absurd mystical readings for Professor Trelawney's Divination class. Hermione uses her intelligence to good effect and her endless stream of knowledge, much of which is invaluable to Harry, comes from her close reading of *Hogwarts – A History*, *An Appraisal of Magical Education in Europe* and similar titles.

Harry's increasing magical powers also come from his education. The spells he learns in different lessons equip him to resist Voldemort. In *Harry Potter and the Prisoner of Azkaban* he is painstakingly taught the Patronus Charm by Professor Lupin, even though it is a magic well beyond his years, because he needs to know how to protect himself against the Dementors; learning the Summoning Charm – the trick of getting what you want to fly into your hand – takes a lot of practice with books, quills and upturned chairs and finally succeeds with a dictionary, but it more than pays off when Harry summons his Firebolt to him in the first task of the Triwizard Tournament in *Harry Potter and the Goblet of Fire*, let alone when it saves his life by allowing him to escape from Voldemort.

CHAPTER 8

Family

Racial and social concerns are the big issues, education is valued and the confined world of school is the main backdrop, but Rowling roots her fantasy firmly within the family. Family background is an issue as it is related to the question of the social hierarchy within the wizarding world but, beyond that, Rowling is more interested in families and what they give each child. As with her creation of a fantasy school community with its detailed networks and interactions closely modelled on the real thing, so Rowling's families are immediately recognizable.

While in descriptive terms Rowling falls readily into caricature when describing family, in emotional terms she is both understanding and caring. At a time of changing patterns of families with decreasing numbers of children being brought up in traditional family structures, Rowling centres the Harry Potter stories around the emotional power base of the Weasley family. Not only the seven Weasley children but Harry and Hermione, too, are sustained by Mr and Mrs Weasley. The security of the Weasley family home appears to act as a traditional yardstick of how families should be. There seem to be no complicated families among Harry's friends: no step-fathers, mothers, brothers or sisters to be accommodated and no difficulties about spending time in two separate homes.

Recognizing that children need to be able to draw on emotional strength to grow up and develop Rowling is careful to provide that strength where necessary. Defining the family relationships of the characters that matter lifts them from the one dimensional and gives them an emotional depth that engages her readers. While few characters have complete families, the additions of brothers and sisters fits convincingly within the school framework and allows a wider range of feelings to develop. This happens through the series with the arrival at Hogwarts of Ginny, the youngest Weasley, in *Harry Potter and the Chamber of Secrets* and Colin Creevey's younger brother Dennis in *Harry Potter and the Goblet of Fire*.

The central juxtaposition, in terms of family love, lies between Harry's unloved situation as an orphan housed by unwilling relatives and Ron's position within an over-large, ebullient and loving family. Ron's abundance of family support and the emotional strength it gives him enable him to support Harry emotionally. Rowling is superficially crude in reflecting the emotional poverty of the Dursleys in their over-orderly domesticity as opposed to the warmth of the Weasleys with their chaotic comings and goings and their over-crowded house. But once past the easily recognized stereotypes, Rowling's detail is compelling.

The Dursleys' self-inflicted unhappiness serves to represent the hazards of too much conformity. Their anxieties are more concerned with what others might think of them than with any notion of what they might themselves enjoy. In direct reference to Roald Dahl's *Matilda* (1988) Rowling is snobbish in her portrait of Middle England, with families more worried about social status than anything else. Status is defined by cars and holidays against a background of deep cultural impoverishment. Love, where it does exist in Vernon and Petunia's devotion to their son Dudley, is shown as indulgent and misplaced. Dudley is over-weight and materialistic: his wealth of birthday presents is designed both to reflect his parents' love for him and his greed. Rowling's caricature is scathing. The extent of Harry's rejection from his unloving home initially serves to define his lot as miserable but, by dismissing the Dursleys so contemptuously, Rowling takes away from Harry's grief. Not being loved by the Dursleys is a blessing as it is clearly not a love worth having.

In contrast, the Weasleys' home is awash with powerful bonds of love and family loyalty. Not as tidy as either of the families of four that make up the Swallows in Arthur Ransome's *Swallows and Amazons* series or the chosen rulers of Narnia, (Peter, Susan, Edmund and Lucy), the Weasleys bear more relationship to the rather chaotic Bastables of E. Nesbit's *Five Children and It* and *The*

Phoenix and the Carpet. Their home has everything a happy home should have: Mrs Weasley cooks large meals, knits ill-shaped jumpers, insists on rubbing smudges off faces, muddles up the names of her children and, above all, gets properly cross when worried – as when Fred and George take their father's car without permission and fly over to collect Harry from the Dursleys. Mildly eccentric, but not alarmingly so, Mr Weasley is guided by Mrs Weasley on all matters of importance.

In Rowling's description of the Weasleys, her stereotypically happy family is hardly less of a fantasy construction than the magic which pops up unexpectedly around it. However, her creation of the individual Weasley children, and especially their complex and natural sibling relationships, saves the perfection which the idea of the family harbours from ever being dull.

Rowling's ability to catch the nuances of family banter, rivalry, frustrations and, above all, solidarity makes the Weasleys critical to the success of the Harry Potter series.

Ostensibly, Ron is depressed by the consequences of having all his older brothers. Not only does he have the indignity of second-hand everything, including an inadequate second-hand wand and a second-hand rat, but he also suffers from the fact that they have already done anything and everything worth doing. Of those still at Hogwarts, Percy is a prefect and Fred and George are the most amusing, dare-devil pair in the school. Of those that have left, one was captain of Quidditch, and one was head boy. Antonia Forest created a similar family structure with the six Marlow sisters in her series *Autumn Term* (1948) and its sequels set in Kingscote School. Both Forest and Rowling use the range of siblings to excellent purpose: older siblings are invaluable for passing on knowledge, especially the kind of detailed knowledge about what happens within a school. As the Harry Potter series unfolds, previous knowledge of Hogwarts becomes more important. Ron, though new to Hogwarts like Harry and Hermione, already knows a lot about it through his older brothers. The combination of coming from an old wizarding family and having considerable and valuable inside knowledge of the school initially gives him a status within the school community which outweighs his poverty.

In the relationships between the six brothers, Rowling shows warmth and humour and an excellent ear for dialogue. While Percy himself is a little shadowy, what he is like is made vivid when he is relentlessly teased. Jokes about him boasting about being made a prefect and endlessly polishing his prefect's badge make excellent and convincing brotherly banter which Rowling sets well against natural maternal pride. In *Harry Potter and the Philosopher's Stone*, Percy pompously announces that he will be at the front of the train where the prefects have two reserved compartments. Fred and George pretend not to know that Percy is a prefect with an elaborate and extended joke, while Mrs Weasley justifies his new robes in recognition of his prefect status.

An older Percy now working for the Ministry of Magic in *Harry Potter and the Goblet of Fire* retains his pomposity when demanding quiet to work on his report on standardizing the thickness of cauldron bottoms and in his obsequiousness towards his boss Mr Crouch. Rowling keeps up the younger brothers' incessant taunts which are invariably witty, if unusually benign for absolute authenticity among brothers.

In Fred and George Weasley, Rowling has created a convincing set of inter-dependent twins: Fred and George are lightweight antidotes to the more serious triumvirate of Harry, Ron and Hermione. They do not engage in the darker magic that dogs the school nor do they use magic for its higher purpose. Their tricks are all jokes and pranks, far removed from the serious art form of magic that Hogwarts is meant to be training them for. Without an ounce of malice in them, fun to be with and good at sport, Fred and George are the classic 'good sort' schoolboys more at home in school-story traditions than in most contemporary schools.

Initially, since *Harry Potter and the Philosopher's Stone* takes place almost entirely within Hogwarts, it is only the brothers at the school who have any significance. The two older brothers, Charlie and Bill are hardly mentioned. Their activity in other spheres of the wizarding world, one in banking and one studying dragons in Romania, expands the map without adding much detail. Ron's younger sister Ginny, still too young to come to Hogwarts, is also a shadowy figure.

As the books continue, Ginny remains a cipher, despite her active role in *Harry Potter and the Chamber of Secrets*, lacking even a striking physical description (except that she has the family red hair) which her brothers are all given. Rowling shies away from giving a perspective on Ginny as the brothers never speak much of her and she has no profile in the school. The references to her – as having a tendency to blush whenever Harry is near – serve only to belittle her.

In *Harry Potter and the Goblet of Fire*, the story with the widest perimeters and the largest non-Hogwarts setting, Harry meets Charlie and Bill for the first time. Charlie's job in working with dragons is confirmed by his burnt arms and healthy tan – obvious signs of an outdoor life. Rowling's description of him is pedestrian with little that immediately marks him out as magical or engages the reader's close interest.

In contrast, with Bill Rowling does what she can do best: creating a character whose skills in wizardry are a witty version of the familiar. Harry knows that Bill works in Gringotts, the wizard bank, and that he had been head boy of Hogwarts. He, and therefore the reader, expects an older version of the bossy Percy combined with a thrusting young city banker in the contemporary image. Instead, Rowling surprises. Bill has a pony tail and one earring – a fang, just to give it a magical touch. To the younger Harry, Bill is the embodiment of cool.

By making Bill a wholly recognizable pastiche of a contemporary young man, reinforced by Mrs Weasley's tut-tutting despair that he won't cut his hair or remove his earring, Rowling makes a secure base from which the magic that surrounds the Weasley household is all the more amusing. Like Hogwarts itself, the overcrowded, jolly Weasley family is familiar as a fictional institution, if not bearing much in common with reality, and the addition of magical touches – potatoes which peel themselves and jump into the pot, garden gnomes who are alive, a clock which tells where different members of the family are – makes it so likeable.

It is as an institution that the Weasleys are so important. The Weasley family, as an emblem of what a happy family should be, grows through the books. Harry's first visit to their house and his immediate inclusion into the family circle give him a new strength and make him particularly receptive to the contacts with his own dead parents.

The contrasting relationships of Harry and Ron to their families are clearly expressed in *Harry Potter and the Philosopher's Stone* when each looks at himself in the Mirror of Erised. They do not know it at the time, though readers decoding the mirror writing will discover, but the mirror will reveal to them what they most want to know. Harry, desperate to know where he comes from, sees a picture of himself with a crowd of people standing around him. The mirror image, like pictures at Hogwarts and elsewhere in the magical world, moves. A pretty woman who, when Harry looks closely, has eyes very like his own appears to wave to him. He also notices that though she is smiling she is also crying. Next to her and with his arm around her is a man with untidy black hair and glasses. Like Harry's, the man's hair sticks up at the back. Gradually Harry realizes that these images are his parents. On looking further into the mirror he sees that others have the same eyes, the same noses, even the same knobbly knees as his own. They are his family, whom he is seeing for the first time in his life, and it brings him a mixture of joy and terrible sadness.

In contrast, Ron is anxious to know that he, too, will do something special to make him feel valued alongside his achieving brothers. The vision he sees in the mirror is of himself not only as head boy but as captain of Quidditch as well. His ambitious dreams are fulfilled.

Harry's emotional growth is dependent on knowing that his parents really loved him. He is sustained and tormented by being able to hear his mother's voice in his dreams when she begs Voldemort to spare him. Once at Hogwarts, he gathers greater sustenance from seeing his parents in the mirror and in photographs given him by Hagrid. From both, his parents wave at him demonstrating their affection. Through all this, Harry can be assured that he was much loved. He can absorb Mrs Weasley's mothering, not as a substitute for his own but as the physical embodiment of what he has lost.

The row that erupts between Harry and Malfoy when Malfoy is derogatory about Mrs Weasley in *Harry Potter and the Goblet of Fire* reflects Harry's identification with the Weasleys. Harry replies by cussing Malfoy's mother in a needle-sharp wizard version of the most acute playground 'cuss'.

The importance of family ties is referred to again and again. Siblings at Hogwarts expect to go into the same house; they support one another in times of need. In Rowling's world of clearly defined right and wrong, good people like Ron come from good and likeable families. Hermione's family, though Muggle and therefore shadowy, is also perfectly acceptable.

In contrast, Malfoy's parents are as disagreeable as might be expected. Harry first meets Lucius Malfoy as he is disposing of illegal goods in Mr Borgin's shop in Knockturn Alley at the beginning of *Harry Potter and the Chamber of Secrets*. Mrs Malfoy doesn't appear until *Harry Potter and the Goblet of Fire* and is crudely dismissed as a blonde, like Draco, who would have been attractive if she didn't have a permanently mean and dissatisfied expression.

Pulls of sibling love and loyalty such as Ron's rescue of Ginny from the Chamber of Secrets and, even more dramatically, in the second task of the Triwizard Tournament in *Harry Potter and the Goblet of Fire* when Fleur, the Beauxbatons champion, has to rescue her sister Gabrielle as she is 'the thing that she will miss most' echo

Peter, Susan and Lucy's part in the rescue of Edmund from the enchantment of the White Witch in C. S. Lewis's *The Lion, the Witch and the Wardrobe*.

The worst thing that can happen within a family is the breakdown of those strong family bonds. In *Harry Potter and the Goblet of Fire* the Crouch family is displayed as wholly dysfunctional. The younger Barty Crouch joined the Death Eaters and forced his father to choose between family loyalty and loyalty to the fight against the Dark Arts. For a father to commit his son to the horrors of Azkaban is portrayed as a truly dreadful crime; for a son to act against his father, let alone to kill him as Barty Crouch does, is unforgivable.

Born as Tom Marvolo Riddle, Voldemort's family background is also telling in contributing to his evil. His mother dies giving birth to him after her Muggle husband has abandoned her on discovering she is a witch. Voldemort is brought up in a Muggle orphanage but later seeks out his father, now living with his elderly parents, and murders all three.

To make the family and family loyalties such a central plank in the Harry Potter novels is another example of the deep traditionalism that runs within them. It provides emotional comfort and reassurance which are so much part of the Harry Potter appeal.

PART 3

Conclusion

CHAPTER 9

The Impact of Harry Potter

Within a year of its publication in 1997 *Harry Potter and the Philosopher's Stone* had become an unprecedented publishing success. Children's books are traditionally slow performers since it takes time first for adults and then for children to adopt and so promote them. Here was a book which was quickly making its mark and, in so doing, was making a statement about what children really enjoy reading. Such a success was bound to have an impact on other children's books, raising questions about their suitability for their audience and their potential.

By the time *Harry Potter and the Goblet of Fire* had been published in July 2000, Harry Potter, the boy wizard from a children's book, had permeated the public consciousness. He and his author had moved far beyond the confines of the children's book world, or even the world of publishing and reading. Their names were currency on quiz shows and in crosswords; he was synonymous with magic and enjoyment for children and adults alike; Rowling had been endowed with the status of a pop star, something most unusual for any author.

A children's book had opened up a new image for readers, new optimism about reading and, in particular, new thinking about what was possible in children's books. Pushed to its limits, it brought about a new approach to children and their culture.

The overwhelming success of the Harry Potter books with children changed the status and image of children's reading. Just as in the 1970s and 1980s Roald Dahl had been an author whose name children knew and whose books they were happy to be seen reading and discussing, so Rowling had moved one step further. Children are now not only happy to be seen reading the Harry Potter books, they are proud of it and their enjoyment is such that they want their parents to share in it too.

The Harry Potter books are accessible stories which cross all reading divides: they are neither too literary nor too popular, too difficult nor too easy, neither too young nor too old. Rowling's clear and predictably structured prose style is particularly praised by those working with dyslexic readers who can read and enjoy these seemingly difficult books. For children especially, but adults too, knowing about Harry Potter's world is important; conversations about the characters and their actions take place freely. For the first time since the arrival of other mass media a series of children's books is holding a cultural position that is a match for a series such as *Friends* or *Neighbours*, something that had seemed unimaginable in an era in which reading, and children's reading in particular, is not especially highly valued beyond the level of a functional literacy.

Harry Potter and the Philosopher's Stone was published at a time when children were perceived in two ways. On the one hand, they were increasingly being pigeon-holed as brattish, selfish, consumerist, uncaring and greedy. In the United Kingdom, a generation of children had grown up in a society in which the notion of community had been systematically eroded while the importance of the common good had been forgotten in the need to strive for materialism and self-promotion. Children were no longer the innocents, eager to please and receptive to imagination. They were demanding and knowing.

On the other hand, childhood, once seen as a time of happiness and freedom, a time of security with expectations of nurture, had changed. Shifting family patterns left some children bewildered and unhappy while parental fears for safety restricted independent activity.

Against this background, many children's books have attempted to give a realistic but optimistic view of contemporary society with its changing domestic, cultural and social patterns. To reflect these new social patterns children's book publishing since the mid–1970s has concentrated, with some notable exceptions, on social realism and emphasized brevity and simplicity of language.

Children's books which played a responsible role in addressing aspects of the society into which they were published had made the issues of reconfigured families central to many stories. Anne Fine's

Madame Doubtfire (1987) and *Goggle Eyes* (1989), which managed to be searingly accurate about how much pain parental break-up caused for children as well as wildly funny, gave rise to a generation of fictions – mostly less amusing – about dealing with step-parents. For a slightly younger audience, Jacqueline Wilson came to dominate the charting of contemporary family life in the 1990s with her moving, mostly first-person narratives in books such as *The Story of Tracy Beaker* (1991), *The Suitcase Kid* (1993) and *Double Act* (1995) among others.

Unrelated, but also a threat to the notion of childhood as an idyll, was the increasing fear for the safety of children. As a result the freedoms of childhood were being eroded. Children operating without adults had once featured prominently in children's books such as Arthur Ransome's *Swallows and Amazons* and its many successors through the decades: most popularly in Enid Blyton's *Famous Five* series (from 1942); in fantasies such as Alan Garner's *The Weirdstone of Brisingamen* (1960) and Penelope Lively's *The Whispering Knights* (1971); and then in World-War-Two fiction, where parents are removed by the vagaries of war, with Nina Bawden's *Carrie's War* (1973) and Robert Westall's *The Machine Gunners* (1975). By the late twentieth century those freedoms were not possible in literature as they might encourage children to take unnecessary risks. Childhood in both reality and stories had become over-protected as fears for children's safety grew.

There were of course exceptions to the diet of social realism. Other fantasies were still being written, just as old-fashioned school stories were endlessly being republished and repackaged. There was widespread enthusiasm among adults and children alike for the reissues of classics, such as Richmal Crompton's *Just William* stories (from 1922) – especially as read on audio tape by Martin Jarvis – and for fantasies such as Eva Ibbotson's *The Secret of Platform 13* (1996), Henrietta Branford's historical *Fire, Bed and Bone* (1997) and Susan Price's historical/science fiction *The Sterkam Handshake* (1998). The devotion of readers to the many volumes of Brian Jacques *Redwall* series (1986–2000) and to Terry Pratchett's fantasy worlds as in *Truckers* (1989) and *Diggers* (1990) showed that despite the media attention devoted to social realism, especially if it could give rise to shocked headlines about sex or drugs in children's books, children were still reading and enjoying other kinds of stories.

Harry Potter was not unique but it was published against what was seen as the most flourishing strand in children's books. At a time when books were mostly being talked about in terms of their message, Rowling's old-fashioned school-story adventure challenged the orthodoxy. Its success showed children enjoying the escapism that Harry Potter offers. Enjoyment of something so simple, so harmless and so witty has had far-reaching effects on attitudes to children's books and even children themselves. It is only a mild overstatement to say that it has given children a new demeanour. Just as Harry, Hermione and Ron are seen as likeable, civilized and interesting and the best of their world is also seen as such, so the effect has been to imbue children with the same desirable characteristics. The brattish, consumer-orientated stereotype is now being countered by the idea that children can be enterprising, honest and resourceful. The conventionality and conformity of the Hogwarts pupils is providing a model for childhood which many find most desirable.

As a publishing phenomenon, nothing as big as Harry Potter has ever happened in children's books, hardly even in adult books. Though publishing, and particularly children's book publishing, is not traditionally seen as being solely profit-driven and books often have a status that relates to their value in terms of literary merit rather than sales, it is – and increasingly so – a business. Harry Potter has changed the face of that business.

The publishers are understandably discreet about exact sales figures and, with the speed at which they continue to mount, round-ups are somewhat meaningless. A few snapshots serve to give a picture of the scale of Harry Potter publishing: four years after the publication of *Harry Potter and the Philosopher's Stone* total world-wide sales of the four Harry Potter titles exceeded 100 million copies. In July 2001, the paperback edition of *Harry Potter and the Goblet of Fire* went into the shops and notched up sales of almost 100,000 in just two days. This came on top of selling 250,000 copies of the same title in hardback on the day when it was published in July 2000. In the week in which the paperback of *Harry Potter and the Goblet of Fire* was published the Harry Potter titles accounted for more than 4% of the total and 28% of the children's books market in terms of revenue. And, in the same week, the four Harry Potter titles continued to occupy the four top spots in the BookTrack Top 10 Children's Books with Rowling's jokey little books published for Red Nose Day – *Fantastic Beasts and Where to Find Them* by Newt Scamander and *Quidditch Through the Ages* by Kennilworthy Whisp taking up the next two. Overall, sales figures of the four Harry Potter titles have hovered around 150,000 per week for the past year.

These sales figures are out of scale with any other children's books. Even Philip Pullman and Jacqueline Wilson, who themselves are both best-selling authors, have sales figures which come nowhere near. The books of Philip Pullman's *His Dark Materials* trilogy have sold in the region of 1 million copies in the UK market since *Northern Lights* was published in 1995. Sales of Jacqueline Wilson's books have averaged about 16,000 per week over the period April to June 2001, but this is across 53 titles.

What the Harry Potter sales figures show is that where there was once apparently a dearth of readers there now seem to be plenty. Obviously, through the combination of her gripping story-telling and her well-timed sense of humour Rowling is making new readers. This overwhelming success has raised expectation of what can be achieved by other books and by other authors. It has also changed the perception of what children like to read.

★★★

Rowling has become an international superstar, attracting the kind of media attention usually reserved for pop stars, film stars, footballers or supermodels. This shift has had an effect on the status of authors and their place in the social hierarchy. It has brought children's literature to the attention of adults and reminded them how rewarding and entertaining it can be. Philip Pullman's *Northern Lights,* published just three years earlier, and the subsequent volumes in the *His Dark Materials* trilogy reinforced this important message. The effect has been that children's books are more likely to be taken as serious contributors to contemporary literature.

More specifically, since the success of *Harry Potter and the Philosopher's Stone* became so apparent, all publishers – and all those working in other media, too – have been looking for other books that might have something of the same compulsion. Anything with magic, fantasy or schools was immediately assumed to be a worthy successor to Harry Potter. Among an output of titles which had previously been concerned primarily with the social issues of the day, this was a significant turnaround. Books carried straplines bearing the message 'If you've enjoyed Harry Potter, you'll certainly enjoy this'. Within the past four years some established writers like Diana Wynne Jones, whose *Crestomanci* stories had been published in the 1970s, have been brought back into prominence with attractive new editions of old titles. Fantasies which Rowling herself was known to have enjoyed such as Elizabeth Goudge's *The Little White Horse* (1946), the story of Maria who stays in a mysterious house in

Cornwall and encounters a magical unicorn, were reissued endorsed with her enthusiasm – enough to attract new readers. New fantasy writers have also benefited from the change of fashion, such as Darren Shan whose *Cirque du Freak* (1999) was hailed as one of the next major fantasies.

Rowling's extraordinary success has been put down to Blooms-bury's clever and persistent marketing. Even though the book's success far outshone its marketing push, what happened to Harry Potter has had a considerable effect on how subsequent major children's titles have been published and marketed.

Unlike adult books, few children's books had been given more than the most gentle marketing. Major authors such as Roald Dahl, Dick King-Smith, Anne Fine and, more recently, Jacqueline Wilson and Philip Pullman had always been successfully promoted by their publishers on a modest scale within the confines of the children's book world, but major campaigns in non-book outlets were almost unheard of. The first TV advertisement for a children's author was made by Puffin for Roald Dahl in the spring of 2001. For the paperback edition of *Harry Potter and the Goblet of Fire* there was a poster campaign on London buses. These two examples are exceptional, but all major new children's books are now backed by a considerable promotion. The most recent and striking example of a book which attracted the new breed of high-profile marketing was *Artemis Fowl* by Eoin Colfer, published in 2001, an engaging action adventure involving fairies, goblins and a great deal of expensive technology. Colfer is one of many whose publisher hopes that he may benefit from some of Rowling's success.

Perhaps more important than how books are published is what Harry Potter has done for children as readers. For some time, publishers have adopted a utilitarian view that the way to find or make readers is to publish to a specific market: the book is defined by its readership rather than by the quality of its writing or the power of its story-telling. The result is books that try to attract new readers, particularly the groups that most obviously have not been readers in the past. These include boys who head the category labelled reluctant readers. Children's reading is now part of the education rather than the recreation agenda. With their knowledge of pupils' needs, schools select books which are pitched at the right level in terms of writing or, since this is what children have always seemed to respond to, contain the right subject matter.

Rowling has stood this wisdom on its head by showing that what children want to read is a good story which also considers some serious issues. She has taken children's reading away from mediating adults. She has shown that children can read and can do so with enthusiasm when the story provides them with imagination, stimulation and emotional nourishment. She has swung the fashion of culture for children away from either a quick fix of instant gratification or a story based in a readily identified reality. She has combined conventionality and traditionalism with magic in a fantasy that is optimistic about children's potential to behave in a likeable and responsible way.

Index

Where the reference to an author is indirect the page number is shown in parentheses.